Mimicking Sisyphus: America's Countervailing Nuclear Strategy

Mimicking Sisyphus: America's Countervailing Nuclear Strategy

Louis René Beres
Purdue University

LexingtonBooks
D.C. Heath and Company
Lexington, Massachusetts
Toronto

Library of Congress Cataloging in Publication Data

Beres, Louis René.
Mimicking Sisyphus : America's countervailing nuclear strategy.

Includes index.
1. Deterrence (Strategy) 2. United States—Military policy. 3. Strategic forces—United States. 4. Strategic forces—Soviet Union. 5. Atomic weapons and disarmament. I. Title.
U162.6.B47 1982 355'.0217'0973 82-48437
ISBN 0-669-06137-9

Published simultaneously in Canada

Printed in the United States of America

Casebound International Standard Book Number: 0-669-06137-9

Paperbound International Standard Book Number: 0-669-06419-x

Library of Congress Catalog Card Number: 82-48437

For Valerie and Lisa

Companions on the return to Jerusalem;
Wellsprings of a continuous redemption.

Contents

Preface

According to Greek myth, the gods condemned Sisyphus to ceaselessly roll a rock to the top of a mountain, whence the stone would fall back of its own weight. In imposing this judgment they understood that there can be no more dreadful punishment than hopeless labor. In the fashion of Sisyphus the United States now labors for national security by wedding its nuclear strategy to a set of futile policies. Unlike Sisyphus, however, this country can avoid an invidious fate by reorienting its labors toward a different path, one that leads not to perpetual and unspeakable torment but to lucidity and safety.

This book points the way to the secure path. My hope in writing it has been sparked by the understanding that avoiding nuclear war, once only a marginal tic of consciousness, is now a swollen, irreversible gesture. Having reached that point in human evolution where our species maintains a perspective on its own gigantic failures, we must exploit that perspective to escape the predatory embrace of collective disintegration. As long as we continue to stand in the ruins of thought—ruins created by generations of strategic planners and their patrons in government—we will be unable to avoid the more tangible ruins of atomic warfare.

"Cogito ergo boom!" Since the end of World War II, this has been the most telling elucidation of America's commitment to strategic thought. Reflecting glib archaeologists of ruins in the making, it degrades the potential for reform of world order to an era of permanent apocalypse. Under its aegis the best and most creative speculation has been put in the service of what Lewis Mumford calls the military "megamachine." With its advent we all (not only our soldiers) are being methodically drawn into a "dreadful ceremony" of worldwide human sacrifice. (See Mumford's *The Myth of the Machine: The Pentagon of Power* [New York: Harcourt Brace Jovanovich, 1964]. In this book, which climaxes a series of studies that began with the publication of *Technics and Civilization* in 1934, Mumford identifies what he calls the "wholesale miscarriages of megatechnics" that have misdirected our human energies and brought us closer to a "permanent state of war.")

Happily, many have begun to understand what is happening. Although we are all still servants of the megamachine, growing numbers of people are beginning to recognize its megalomanic and paranoid distortion of reality. Casting aside ritual trust in "peace through strength," they have begun to invest a growing consciousness with action. Rejecting the rules of conduct that had divided them from their own possibilities, they now contemplate the dénouement of planetary political life with a new deportment, one in which the impetuous void of current strategic plans is replaced by the clarity and coherence of less vertiginous thoughts. I am thinking especially of those scholars and public figures who write against the countervailing nuclear strategy and of those participants in the expanding movements for European and worldwide nuclear disarmament. The pertinent names will appear throughout this book.

"Sapere Aude!" Dare to know! This motto of the Enlightenment offered by Kant has acquired a special meaning in the repudiation of current programs for a "countervailing" nuclear strategy. Having taken civilization seriously, an enlarged body of conscious individuals stands before the purveyors of strategic myth, countering their exhibitions of uninformed effrontery and old arrogances with prudence and genuine understanding. In so doing, they have given new meaning to Samuel Beckett's question: "What is the good of passing from one untenable position to another, of seeking justification always on the same plane?"

This meaning, from our point of view, must concern the futility of seeking peace through unending refinements of nuclear overkill. There exist at the present moment at least 40,000 to 50,000 nuclear weapons in world arsenals, carrying explosive power equivalent to more than 1 million Hiroshima bombs. Since this amounts to more than 13 billion tons of TNT, it represents more than 3 tons for every man, woman, and child on earth. The arsenals of the United States and the Soviet Union contain most of these weapons: the United States has over 9,000 strategic nuclear weapons; the Soviet Union about 7,000.

Over the years the competitive production of these nuclear weapons has proceeded relentlessly, unmindful of the fact there can be no conceivable justification for piling weapon upon weapon, missile upon missile. More recently the already precarious situation has been aggravated by a steady doctrinal shift in American thinking about nuclear strategy. Inexplicably this shift, by deemphasizing minimum deterrence as the singular rationale of strategic policy, has produced a counterforce syndrome that gives apparent legitimacy to the idea of nuclear war fighting. In the words of Leon Sloss, who directed this country's nuclear targeting policy review for the Department of Defense in 1978: "The emphasis has shifted from the *survivability* necessary to assure that we can launch a single preplanned strike to the *endurance* necessary to actually fight a war that may extend over some period of time and involve a series of nuclear exchanges." (See Leon Sloss, "Carter's Nuclear Policy: Going from '*MAD*' to Worse? No: It's Evolutionary, Not Revolutionary, and Aims to Strengthen Deterrence," Los Angeles Times, August 31, 1980, p. 3. Emphasis in original.)

Before we can pass from the untenable position involved in this shift to a more promising plane of international understanding, we must learn to recognize that what is currently called "strategic thinking" is the antithesis of genuine thought, a pathetic caricature of America's potential for building a reliable structure of peace. Accepting a fatality without substance as operational doctrine, this supposed thinking substitutes the *hauteur* of primacy for prudent mental activity. As the handmaiden of an insipid nuclear theology, it offers clichés and stock phrases that serve only to blind us to the truth. In this respect the strategic thinking is illustrated nicely by Beckett's play, *Waiting for Godot*, when Lucky, who, at his master's order to "Think," can only sputter out a long speech that has all the pomposity of academic discourse but is actually pure gibberish.

We are already almost lost in our own gibberish. By making its assertions without regard for what is known, this gibberish seeks by din and repetition to make opposition impossible. Before this situation can be reversed, our strategic planners will have to abandon their models of circular sophistry in favor of more broadly reasoned patterns. Instead of old arguments repeated again and again with the stereotyped monotony of schizophrenic dreams, the Reagan administration will have to open its mind to ways of understanding not yet its own.

America has been thinking against itself. To survive into the future, it will require a new consciousness—one tuned to ever higher pitches of strategic refinement. To avoid further contamination by the superstitions of those who urge expanding patterns of nuclear militarization, America must resist confronting the *Apocalypse* as healer. Its sole ambition must be to prevent the incurable.

Wrote Andrei Sakharov in *Progress, Coexistence, and Intellectual Freedom*, "A thermonuclear war cannot be considered a continuation of politics by other means [Carl von Clausewitz's characterization of war]. . . . It would be a means of universal suicide." Rather than continue to portray nuclear war as an ordinary political "option" (a portrayal that Clausewitz would clearly find abhorrent), the United States must hew to a paradigm of strategic thinking based on the absolute rejection of nuclear war fighting as a rational instrument of national policy. At a time when the classical system of world politics is undergoing the most profound metamorphoses, national leaders must learn to replace the dying forms of power politics with an altogether new form of national consciousness.

A few years after the Declaration of Independence, the Continental Congress adopted as a motto on the great seal of the United States a phrase of Virgil's: *Novus Ordo Seclorum* (A new age beginning). In a world imperiled by the irreversible grotesquerie of nuclear war, it is time for this motto to be applied to American nuclear strategy. In a world where the convulsive changes in our era signal the possibility of gigadeath, death in the billions, it is time to substitute the dignity of cooperative international interaction for the folly of untrammeled mortal competition. By its actions to make such substitution possible, the United States would carry within itself the potential to confront the ancien régime of militaristic statecraft not as a victim but as a gifted elegist.

Acknowledgments

I am grateful to the Transnational Academic Program (TAP) of the Institute for World Order for providing a fellowship in World Order Studies and for offering continued encouragement of my work on U.S. nuclear strategy. In this connection, I owe a particular debt to Sherle Schwenninger, director of the TAP, who has been a steady source of intellectual support and wise counsel. I am also indebted to my editor at Lexington Books, Marilyn Weinstein, for her skillful supervision of the project and for sharing my enthusiasm about its argument. Special thanks are also due to Pamela J. Walch, marketing manager at Lexington Books, for her efforts on behalf of bringing the book before the widest possible audience; to Jaime Welch for her patience and prudence as editorial assistant; to Kathleen Benn for guiding the manuscript expertly through the intricacies of production; and to Cynthia Insolio Benn for her meticulous refinements of the work as copy-editor. By their contributions to this book, these people and programs have made it possible for me to communicate the understanding that it is not possible to imagine Sisyphus happy.

1 Tilting toward Thanatos

From its very beginnings, the Reagan administration has pursued a refractory nuclear strategy that identifies American security with a provocative emphasis on counterforce targeting (a strategy that emphasizes targeting of an adversary's military capability, especially its strategic military capability) and renewed arms racing. Threatening to undermine the already fragile foundations of a peace based on reciprocal threats of obliteration, this policy is designed to fulfill military tasks at a level far exceeding the requirements of "minimum deterrence." Building upon the foundations of Presidential Directive 59 signed by President Carter on July 25, 1980,[1] the Reagan nuclear policy goes beyond the legitimate objective of survivable and penetration capable strategic forces to steadily accelerated preparations for nuclear war fighting.

The essential rationale of this policy is twofold: First, it is expected to strengthen nuclear deterrence. Faced with what is perceived as a relentless buildup and refinement of Soviet strategic forces and with an adversary that is allegedly preparing for nuclear war, the administration suggests a compelling need for rejecting the principles of Mutual Assured Destruction (MAD). Rather than be faced with an intolerable choice between all-out nuclear war and surrender, it argues, the United States requires a set of "intermediate" retaliatory options. These options have already been incorporated into plans that stress the enlarged destruction of Soviet command authorities and the deployment of long-range theater nuclear forces in Europe.

Second, the Reagan nuclear policy is expected to permit American forces to prevail if deterrence fails. Anticipated by former Secretary of Defense Harold Brown's statement that "we are necessarily giving greater attention to how a nuclear war would actually be fought by both sides if deterrence fails,"[2] this policy counsels preparations for a nuclear war that may be protracted and carefully controlled. Apparently accepting the position of certain think-tank analysts that war at any level can be won or lost and that the United States "must possess the ability to wage nuclear war rationally,"[3] this policy reflects the understanding that a combination of counterforce targeting, crisis relocation of urban populations, and ballistic missile defense could make nuclear war tolerable.

Regrettably, both parts of the policy rationale are misconceived. Based upon a series of erroneous assumptions and upon disregard for synergistic effects between American and Soviet strategies, they codify a set of initiatives that can only hasten the arrival of nuclear war. Unsullied by the reality that the delicate balance of terror cannot endure indefinitely, they compel the USSR to match each American move with an escalatory countermove. The resultant folie à deux can only heighten the insecurities of each superpower. It can never produce peace.

Examined from the standpoint of conventional logic, the basic assumptions of the Reagan administration's nuclear policy are logically irrelevant to their conclusions and therefore incapable of establishing their truth. As in the case of any fallacy the argument may appear to be correct but is actually in error. For example, the policy's plan to secure Soviet "good behavior" by the threat of engaging in a nuclear war is a unique case of the *argumentum ad baculum*. This appeal to force is not only intrinsically unrelated to the merits of the desired course of Soviet conduct, it is also destined to fail.

In a world of international anarchy states have traditionally relied on the *argumentum ad baculum* as a unilateral or collaborative mode of producing security. Although such reliance on war or the threat of war has always been logically irrelevant to the merits of the behavior a state may have been attempting to influence, it has at times been very persuasive. This is no longer the case between the superpowers, however, since neither one can make good on a threat to initiate nuclear war without anticipating an unacceptably damaging retaliation. Such a threat can be manifestly counterproductive, moreover, generating great apprehension and insecurity and thus encouraging a preemptive nuclear strike.

A second fallacy exhibited by the Reagan nuclear policy concerns manipulation of public opinion for domestic political considerations. Here the correctness or reasonableness of the policy is defended by an emotional appeal "to the people" for sustaining defense expenditures of $1.6 trillion over the subsequent five years as a patriotic duty. Describing the massive buildup of Soviet strategic forces as proof positive of their aggressive designs,[4] President Reagan has told the American people that the Soviets will "lie, cheat, and commit any crime" to further their objectives. This appeal to the gallery seeks widespread assent to a conclusion about our nuclear policy that is unsupported by valid argument. A favorite device of the propagandist the *argumentum ad populum* is being used by the administration to mobilize public support for a policy that cannot be supported by rational argument. Popular acceptance of a policy does not prove it to be wise,[5] and before the administration's nuclear policy can be endorsed because of its security benefits it will need to rely less on brass bands and more on reasoned evaluation.

Ironically, the Reagan administration's justification for increased military spending to "rearm America" is one that has been heard again and again since the start of the nuclear arms race. In the early 1950s it was the "bomber gap" that provided the necessary rationale. In the Kennedy era it was the "missile gap." More recently it has been the "vulnerability gap"—together with allegations of rapidly rising Soviet military expenditures and of Soviet inclinations to nuclear war-fighting doctrines of deterrence—that fuels our debilitating pattern of defense spending.

Dramatic estimates of Soviet military spending over the years have been based less upon the discovery of new or accelerated Soviet weapons programs than on new ways of calculating the burden of defense expenditures on the Soviet economy. According to Richard J. Barnet, recurring alarm over the "spending gap" illustrates some of the Alice-in-Wonderland aspects of the nuclear arms race:

> American insecurity rises with the dollars we impute to the Soviet military effort. But in fact actual Soviet expenditures are not known. The U.S. intelligence community reconstructs the Soviet military budget by asking: "What would it cost to buy the Soviet defense establishment in the United States at U.S. prices?" Our intelligence analysts pretend that the Soviets procure their tanks from General Motors and that they pay U.S. volunteer wages to their conscripts.[6]

By computing Soviet manpower costs at U.S. rates, our government has discovered a huge Soviet manpower budget that exists only in American documents.

Here are some additional facts about comparative military expenditures and systems supplied by Admiral Gene R. LaRocque (Ret.) of the Center for Defense Information:

> The U.S, and its NATO allies have outspent the Soviet/Warsaw Pact military forces for many years—$215 billion to $175 billion in one year alone.
>
> The cost of new and often unnecessary weapons continues to escalate. This year the Pentagon says the cost of 47 weapon systems will be $50 billion higher than its estimate for the same weapons in 1980.
>
> The massive U.S. Navy exceeds the Soviets in warship tonnage and nuclear-powered submarines and ships, and outnumbers the Soviets in aircraft carriers by 13 to 0. Now we are building 110 new warships.
>
> Our submarines carry 5,000 nuclear weapons—3,000 of which are always aimed and ready to fire at the USSR. The Soviets keep 400 nuclear weapons at sea, ready to fire at the U.S.
>
> The United States has 410 strategic bombers, compared to the Soviet's 145. More than half of the Soviet bombers are still propeller-driven.
>
> We have *always* had more nuclear weapons than the Soviets. Today we can explode 12,000 nuclear weapons on the Soviet Union, while they can explode 8,000 on us.

> The United States will build 17,000 new nuclear weapons in the 1980's, if we continue to move forward with current plans for the MX, Cruise, Trident, Pershing II, and other weapons.[7]

Since the end of World War II, the United States has spent more than $2 trillion on "defense." Yet today we are almost entirely indefensible. This is the case because no reliable defense exists against nuclear missiles. All of the old rules of warfare have been rendered obsolete; the idea of military superiority has become meaningless. It follows that each escalation of the arms race serves only to *decrease* our security. And this is true whether the escalation is initiated by the United States or by the USSR.

Why is American nuclear superiority unattainable? Why, in the current nuclear world of the superpowers, does "superiority" have no meaning? An answer has been provided by Admiral Noel Gayler, U.S. Navy (Ret.):

> We and Russia are like two riverboat gamblers sitting across a green table, each with a gun pointed at the other's belly and each gun on hair trigger. The size of the guns doesn't make much difference; if either weapon is used, both gamblers are dead. In the same way, the size of the nuclear forces makes little difference. States of readiness, targeting decisions, even which way the wind is blowing (carrying nuclear fallout), make a greater difference than a thousand extra missiles on either side.[8]

What we have today is nuclear parity—a stalemate neither side can break without commiting suicide. The piling of one weapon system upon another gives neither side even one iota of military advantage. It only aggravates the tensions that can lead to miscalculation and oblivion.

The supporters of current American nuclear policy have transmitted to their argument an increasingly rapid circular movement. In the fashion of a quickly spun multicolored disk whose colors interpenetrate to produce white, in this argument appearance *tries* to pass for reality. Unless the confusion becomes widely understood and soon, this country's reaction to the threat of nuclear war will bring us even closer to fulfillment of that threat.

Just how well-founded is President Reagan's search for a margin of safety? According to a recent major statement by General David C. Jones, U.S. Air Force, former chairman of the joint chiefs of staff:

> The flexibility and survivability inherent in the strategic TRIAD concept have stood the test of time, but the forces themselves are seriously in need of modernization. A very serious weapon system concern is the growing vulnerability of our land-based/ICBM force, the key contributor to our time-urgent hard target kill capability. Without a high degree of survivability afforded by the MX missile system, the deterrence and crisis stabiiity of this most precisely controllable component of our strategic force mix could be seriously compromised.[9]

Yet, in his assessment of ICBM vulnerability, General Jones seems to ignore the conditions that would prevail in any real exchange of strategic nuclear weapons. Although it is almost certainly true that a fixed silo and missile, placed under attack from an accurate weapon of very high yield, will be vulnerable, the practical problems of developing a targeting plan that would assure such vulnerability among about 1000 such ICBMs are overwhelming. These problems include probabilities of arrival of the attacking weapons; compounded by probabilities of self-destruction; compounded by probabilities of fratricide, timing, and targeting difficulties. Moreover, since U.S. solid fuel-propelled MM ICBMs can be launched against the Soviet Union well within the thirty minute flight time of Soviet missiles, Soviet weapons launched against U.S. ICBMs might find only empty silos. And even if it could be assumed that the Soviet Union were able to get on a very high side of a damage expectancy curve against U.S. ICBMs, their first-strike—in order to be rational—must also have a high degree of assurance against U.S. submarines and bombers. That kind of capability, of course, is unavailable for the forseeable future at the very least.

Similarly in testimony before the Senate committee on foreign relations, Rear Admiral Eugene Carroll, Jr., U.S. Navy (Ret.), speaking for the Center for Defense Information, expressed apprehension that "the move away from the concept of nuclear deterrence to nuclear warfighting, coupled with the administration's strong anti-Soviet rhetoric and theater nuclear force modernization program . . . is increasing the risk of nuclear war in the world." Continuing with a well-documented assault on the administration's presumption of ICBM vulnerability, Admiral Carroll went on to identify the dangers of the decision to go ahead with MX and to articulate the only reasonable rationale for nuclear weapons:

> Nuclear weapons today serve only one legitimate purpose, to deter nuclear war. The only true test of the sufficiency of our nuclear systems is that they are able to meet any Soviet attack at a level which denies any possible expectation of gain. The present U.S. capability to deliver 12,000 nuclear weapons on the Soviet Union more than meets this test of sufficiency.[10]

Admiral Carroll's concerns are echoed by the former director of the U.S. National Security Agency, Admiral Gayler, who observed:

> What many Americans do not understand is that there is no sensible military use for any of the three categories of nuclear weapons—strategic (of intercontinental range), or theater (capable of reaching targets within one's theater of military operations) or tactical (designed, like atomic cannon, for battlefield use). I say this as a military man, a former commander in chief of all United States forces in the Pacific, an aviator and mariner, soldier and intelligence officer of 46 years' experience.[11]

And in the same vein Vice-Admiral John Marshall Lee, U.S. Navy (Ret.), has stated:

> Our basic military strategy against the USSR is wrong, fundamentally wrong. Recent concepts make it, if anything, worse. That strategy depends, at the end, on using nuclear weapons—on starting, ourselves, the use of nuclear weapons. But, quite simply, nuclear weapons cannot do the job. For rational human purposes, they won't work.[12]

As these analyses suggest, the U.S. search for a margin of safety in strategic capability vis-à-vis the USSR rests upon a misunderstanding of deterrence. In spite of President Reagan's formal commitments to arms control (the United States is now engaged in talks concerning strategic arms reduction, control of intermediate-range nuclear forces in Europe, and mutual balanced force reductions in Europe), the search continues with undiminished zeal. Evidence that this is indeed the case lies not only in the administration's rededication to expanded countersilo capabilities, but also in Secretary of Defense Weinberger's June 3, 1982, confirmation that the United States had adopted a strategy for protracted nuclear war with the USSR. And it lies in the administration's refusal to parallel the USSR's renunciation of the right to "first use" of nuclear weapons, a renunciation pledged by Soviet Foreign Minister Gromyko before the United Nations' second special session on disarmament.

We are confronted with a growing gap between rhetoric and reality. Although the Reagan administration has signaled a de jure commitment to the principles of arms control, this commitment has been accompanied by a continuing American force "revitalization" and by the demand for disproportionate reductions by the USSR. Hardly an appropriate platform for bilateral give and take, the Reagan program is bound to "prove" Soviet intransigence and preclude promising counterproposals.

Where are we heading? The direction seems to be unrestrained nuclear competition. Vitalized by an exaggeratedly tragic expectation of Soviet intentions, this competition will lead to the expression of all of the poison and impotence of American foreign policy since World War II. In its drowning of any remaining hopes for long-term cooperative security with the USSR, it will offer a routinization of humanicide that may ultimately project Armageddon from imagination to reality.

Curiously nothing in our current nuclear strategy suggests a plausible connection between nuclear war and politics. Why, exactly, are the Soviets getting ready to "fight and win" a nuclear war with the United States?[13] What conceivable postwar prospect can be associated with alleged Soviet plans for a first strike against the United States? The Soviets are not likely to act counter to the following principle, stated by Carl Von Clausewitz:

> War is only a branch of political activity; it is in no sense autonomous . . . [It] cannot be divorced from political life—and whenever this occurs in our thinking about war, the many links that connect the two elements are destroyed, and we are left with something that is pointless and devoid of sense.[14]

The dangers of assessing Soviet nuclear intentions in a vacuum are considerable. By assuming that their *Staatspolitik* offers no homage to plausible relationships between nuclear war and national political goals, our own nuclear policy creates a bewildering expectation of first-strike scenarios that in turn produces a staggering array of provocative tactics and deployments. The combined effect of such American strategic thinking is a heightened prospect of escalation and irrevocable collision.

Reflecting Clausewitz's framework for reconciling military strategy with political objectives, Michael Howard, Regius professor of modern history at Oxford University, recently raised important questions about this country's penchant for identifying Soviet intentions with capabilities:

> When I read the flood of scenarios in strategic journals about first-strike capabilities, counterforce or countervailing strategies, flexible response, escalation dominance and the rest of the postulates of nuclear theology, I ask myself in bewilderment: this war they are describing, *what is it about*? The defense of Western Europe? Access to the Gulf? The protection of Japan? If so, why is this goal not mentioned, and why is the strategy not related to the progress of the conflict in these regions? But if it is not related to this kind of specific object, what are we talking about? Has not the bulk of American thinking been exactly what Clausewitz described—something that, because it is divorced from any political context, is "pointless and devoid of sense"?[15]

A corollary of the kind of American strategic thinking described by Howard concerns the alleged Soviet willingness to accept far higher levels of fatalities and destruction in a nuclear war than the United States. This argument is typically drawn from the understanding that the USSR lost 20 million people, 12 percent of its total population, during World War II, and was able to emerge as a stronger nation. As it has been expressed by Richard Pipes, formerly chairman of "Team B," a committee appointed in 1976 by the president's foreign intelligence board to prepare an alternative to the Central Intelligence Agency's assessment of Soviet strategic objectives, and currently a Soviet specialist on the National Security Council, the argument goes something like this:

> Allowing for the population growth which has occurred since then [the end of World War II] this experience suggests that as of today the USSR could absorb the loss of 30 million of its people and be no worse off, in terms of

> human casualties, than it had been at the conclusion of World War II. In other words, all of the USSR's multimillion cities could be destroyed without trace of survivors, and, provided that its essential cadres had been saved, it would emerge less hurt in terms of casualties than it was in 1945.[16]

This argument, like current American nuclear strategy as a whole, is riddled with incorrect reasoning. Assuming that Soviet leaders base their decisions on a careful comparison of the costs and benefits of alternative courses of action (the standard assumption of rationality), what conceivable configuration of benefits could justify the loss of 30 million of its people? Even if such a loss could be absorbed without creating conditions that are worse than those endured at the end of World War II, what reason is there to believe that the USSR would purposely take actions that would permit millions of human casualties? Clearly the fact that such a loss might have historical parallel for the USSR does not automatically imply the rationality of taking steps to ensure its replication. There is in short no reason to suppose that Soviet encouragement of such a loss could ever be considered gainful. As a leading spokesman of the administration's strategic mythmakers, Pipes offers an argument that is founded on the presumed incapacity of Soviet leaders to make rational decisions. Were this assumption taken seriously in the formulation of this country's own strategic policies, it would immobilize the entire logic of nuclear deterrence and occasion rational arguments for preemption by the United States.

Moreover, the assumption that the USSR could emerge from a strategic exchange with the United States "less hurt in terms of casualties than it was in 1945" is entirely erroneous. In the first place this assumption rests on the premise that a superpower nuclear war could be kept "limited," that various targeting and defense measures would be effective in holding down the number and intensity of casualties. Ironically this premise is contradicted not only by a long tradition of Soviet rejection of limited nuclear war thinking[17] but also by Richard Pipes himself: "In the Soviet view, a nuclear war would be total . . . Limited nuclear war, flexible response, escalation, damage limiting, and all the other numerous refinements of the U.S. strategic doctrine find no place in its Soviet counterpart."[18] Moreover, even if we were able to accept the plausibility of limited nuclear war, there is now an overwhelming array of medical and scientific evidence that *nothing* could be done to reduce the number or seriousness of casualties.[19]

In the second place the assumption that the USSR could emerge from a nuclear exchange with the United States "less hurt in terms of casualties than it was in 1945" does not mean that it would emerge "less hurt" in other terms. And these other terms might well be an even more important standard than number of casualties in determining the direction of Soviet strategic objectives. Special reference must be made to the fact that the Soviet capacity for postwar recovery would be far more limited today than it was after World War II. This is the case because today's Soviet economic and industrial base is vastly more complex and vital than it was in 1945.

Since the centrally planned economy of the USSR is now concentrated in a limited number of facilities, it has many vulnerable choke points. Should these facilities be destroyed by American missiles, the return to status quo ante bellum would be far more difficult than it was after World War II. Indeed, even if we were to disregard these choke points, Soviet recovery from a nuclear war with the United States would entail a return to far more advanced conditions of development than was necessary in 1945.

As if these erroneous assumptions and incorrect inferences were not enough to demonstrate the inadequacy of current American nuclear strategy, the Reagan administration has founded this strategy on a series of even more patent violations of correct reasoning. These offenses to logical sensibility involve both additional unwarranted assumptions and disregarded synergistic effects. Taken together, these problematic assumptions and ignored interactions constitute a pyramid of fantasies ready to collapse like a house of cards in the face of reasoned evaluation.

Notes

1. Presidential Directive 59 was clarified by former Secretary of Defense Harold Brown in a speech at the Naval War College on August 20, 1980. Derived from a war plan known as National Security Decision Memorandum 242 formulated in the closing months of the Ford administration, the directive represents a major retreat from the doctrine of "massive retaliation" first defined by John Foster Dulles in January 1954. The Reagan administration's so-called countervailing nuclear strategy actually goes beyond the principles of PD 59 in its advocacy of "atomic superiority" and its overriding commitment to build a capacity to fight nuclear wars at any level. At present the essential elements of this strategy are embedded in a five-year defense plan initiated by Secretary of Defense Weinberger in spring 1982 to expand United States strategic nuclear forces so that they might meet the requirements of nuclear war fighting. According to *The New York Times*, the defense guidance plan states: "The United States nuclear capability must prevail even under the conditions of a prolonged war. . . . The armed forces must have enough nuclear ability so that the United States would never emerge from a nuclear war without nuclear weapons while still threatened by enemy nuclear weapons." Reflecting the strategists' notion of "escalation dominance," the document goes on to say that American nuclear forces "must prevail and be able to force the Soviet Union to seek earliest termination of hostilities on terms favorable to the United States" (Richard Halloran, "New Atom War Strategy Confirmed," *The New York Times*, June 4, 1982, p. 7). It is conceivable, of course, that

such administration pronouncements are merely rhetoric and that current strategy for the actual employment of nuclear weapons is substantially the same as it has been for some time. This may well be the case because the proof of any policy lies in its implementation, in the directives sent through the bureaucracy to the implementers, and it is not certain that the administration has provided the necessary implementation for its strategic plans. At the same time it would be foolhardy to conclude that these plans are intended only for political consumption and that they ought to be discounted. The central document in U.S. strategic nuclear targeting policy is known as the Single Integrated Operations Plan (SIOP). The first SIOP was put together in late 1960. The Nuclear Weapons Employment Policy (NUWEP) is the secretary of defense's guide to the joint chiefs of staff for use of American nuclear weapons. On the basis of such guidance, the joint chiefs prepare a more specific guidance to the joint strategic target planning staff, which in turn prepares detailed operational plans for the employment of our nuclear weapons.

2. Harold Brown, remarks delivered at the Convocation Ceremonies for the 97th Naval War College Class, Newport, Rhode Island, August 20, 1980, p. 6.

3. See Colin Gray and Keith Payne, "Victory Is Possible," *Foreign Policy* 39 (Summer 1980): 14. Although Secretary of Defense Weinberger seems to have moved away from the "victory is possible" position with his speech at the U.S. Army War College on June 3, 1982 (a speech that asserted that nowhere in President Reagan's $180 billion program to "revitalize" the nuclear deterrent "do we mean to imply that nuclear war is winnable"), the elements of this speech stand in marked contrast with his defense guidance document (on strategy for fighting a "protracted" nuclear war). Although this document was conceived with a view to avoiding nuclear war by strengthening deterrence, this view is founded upon the presumed advantages of the strategy of escalation dominance—the ability to "prevail" under conditions of a protracted nuclear war. There is no reason to believe that such an ability would place additional constraints on any Soviet incentives to strike first, but there is reason to believe that it might remove existing constraints by signaling renewed American provocativeness. And there is reason to believe that the repeated emphasis on American nuclear capabilities that can prevail reflects no more than a semantic departure from earlier references to victory.

4. In this connection the following statement by Bernard Brodie may be sobering: "Where the Committee on the Present Danger . . . speaks of 'the brutal momentum of the massive Soviet strategic arms buildup—a buildup without precedent in history,' it is speaking of something which no student of the American strategic arms buildup in the sixties could possibly consider unprecedented" (from Brodie's "Development of Nuclear Strategy," *International Security* 2, no. 4 (Spring 1978): 65–83).

5. Increasing evidence reveals that the Reagan policy does not enjoy widespread public support.

6. Quoted from p. 17 of Barnet's *Real Security: Restoring American Power in a Dangerous Decade* (New York: Simon and Schuster, 1981).

7. See "What Price Security?" A Personal Message from Admiral Gene R. LaRocque, Director of the Center for Defense Information, Washington, D.C., 1982.

8. From p. 48 of Gayler's "How to Break the Momentum of the Nuclear Arms Race," *The New York Times Magazine*, April 25, 1982, © 1982 by The New York Times Company. Reprinted by permission.

9. From p.iv of *United States Military Posture for FY 1982*, An Overview by General David C. Jones (Washington, D.C.: U.S. Government Printing Office, 1981).

10. From p. 139 of Testimony on "Strategic Weapons Proposals," Hearings before the Committee on Foreign Relations, U.S. Senate, 97th Congress, First Session, on "The Foreign Policy and Arms Control Implications of President Reagan's Strategic Weapons Proposals," Washington, D.C.: U.S. Government Printing Office, November 9, 1981.

11. "How to Break the Momentum of the Nuclear Arms Race," *The New York Times Magazine*, April 25, 1982, p. 48, © 1982 by The New York Times Company. Reprinted with permission.

12. Stated in remarks before the St. Petersburg, Florida, chapter of the Navy League titled "We Must Change Our Strategy," December 17, 1981.

13. This assessment, endorsed by Vice President Bush during the 1980 presidential election campaign is now embedded in Secretary Weinberger's defense guidance plan, and is seen regularly in the journal and popular literature. See, for example, Leon Sloss's comment that "All the evidence suggests that we confront an adversary who appears to believe it is possible to fight and win a nuclear war." (Commentary on my article "Presidential Directive 59: A Critical Assessment," *Parameters* 11, no. 1 (March 1981): 19–28, appearing in *Parameters*, 11 no. 2 (June 1981): 90. Mr. Sloss, now with SRI International, directed the nuclear targeting policy review for the Department of Defense in 1978. See also Richard Pipes, "Why the Soviet Union Thinks It Could Fight and Win a Nuclear War," *Commentary* 64, no. 1 (July 1977); and Gray and Payne, "Victory Is Possible," pp. 14–27. In fact, no evidence exists that the USSR is preparing to "fight and win" a nuclear war, if by this assessment we mean that country is preparing to make the first strike. Rather, all of the evidence suggests that the USSR, in *response* to any use of nuclear weapons by the United States, would employ the full range of its nuclear options—that it would not engage in the kind of "limited" nuclear war envisioned by American strategic policy. Indeed Soviet spokesmen reflect the understanding that any nuclear war would be intolerable and that there would be no purpose in fighting and winning such a war. In a speech before the twenty-sixth congress of the

Soviet Communist party on February 23, 1981, Leonid Brezhnev said: "To try and outstrip each other in the arms race, or to expect to win a nuclear war, is dangerous madness." In a speech at a Kremlin rally on November 6, 1981, Marshal Dmitri F. Ustinov, Minister of Defense, stated: "Western politicians and strategists stubbornly push the thesis that Soviet military doctrine allegedly assumes the possibility of an 'initial disarming strike,' of survival, and even of victory, in a nuclear war. All this is a deliberate lie." And in an address at a Soviet–American seminar in Washington on January 12, 1982, Nikolai N. Inozemtsev, Director of the Soviet Institute of World Economy and International Relations, observed: "Political and military doctrines have been changed. This has been reflected in our internal life. There is new determination to seek sharp reductions."

14. From Clausewitz's *On War* (Princeton, N.J.: Princeton University Press, 1976), Book 8, ch. 6B, "War Is an Instrument of Policy."

15. From p. 9 of Howard's "On Fighting a Nuclear War," *International Security* 5, no. 4 (Spring 1981): 9. Copyright 1981 by the President and Fellows of Harvard College and the Massachusetts Institute of Technology. Reprinted from *International Security* by permission.

16. See Pipes, "Why the Soviet Union Thinks It Could Fight and Win a Nuclear War," p. 34.

17. See, for example, an early article by Colonel V. Mochalov and Major V. Dashichev, "The Smoke Screen of the American Imperialists," *Red Star*, December 17, 1957; Bernard Brodie, *Strategy in the Missile Age* (Princeton, N.J.: Princeton University Press, 1959), p. 322 n.; R. Simonyan, "Comments," *Strategic Review* 5 (Spring 1977); 100; and the recent remarks of Soviet Lieutenant General Mikhail A. Milshtein, director of the Political-Military Department of the Institute on the United States of America and Canada, cited on p. 8 of "Limited Nuclear War: The Moscow Approach," *The New York Times*, December 7, 1980.

18. See Pipes, "Why the Soviet Union Thinks It Could Fight and Win a Nuclear War," p. 30.

19. There is now a great deal of authoritative information available to support this assessment. See, for example, *Hiroshima and Nagasaki: The Physical, Medical, and Social Effects of the Atomic Bombings*, by the Committee for the Compilation of Materials on Damage Caused by the Atomic Bombs in Hiroshima and Nagasaki (New York: Basic Books, 1981), 706 pp.; *The Final Epidemic*, physicians and scientists on the medical and environmental consequences of nuclear war (*The Bulletin of the Atomic Scientists* [October 1981], 252 pp.); Arthur M. Katz, *Life after Nuclear War* (Cambridge, Mass.: Ballinger, 1981), 452 pp.; "The First Nuclear War Conference," December 7, 1978, a special report of *The Bulletin of the Atomic Scientists* (1979), 43 pp.; *Analyses of Effects of Limited Nuclear Warfare*, a report prepared for the Subcommittee on Arms Control, International Organizations, and Security Agreements of the Committee on For-

eign Relations, U.S. Senate, September 1975, 156 pp.; *Worldwide Effects of Nuclear War . . . Some Perspectives*, a report of the U.S. Arms Control and Disarmament Agency (n.d., but produced after 1975), 24 pp,; *Long-Term Worldwide Effects of Multiple Nuclear-Weapons Detonations*, a report by the Committee to Study the Long-Term Worldwide Effects of Multiple Nuclear-Weapons Detonations, National Academy of Sciences, Washington, D.C., 1975, 212 pp.; *The Effects of Nuclear War*, a report by the Office of Technology Assessment, U.S. Congress, Washington, D.C., May 1979, 151 pp.; *Economic and Social Consequences of Nuclear Attacks on the United States*, a study prepared for the Joint Committee on Defense Production, U.S. Congress, published by the Committee on Banking, Housing, and Urban Affairs, U.S. Senate, Washington, D.C., March 1979, 150 pp.; Kevin N. Lewis, "The Prompt and Delayed Effects of Nuclear War," *Scientific American* 241, no. 1 (July 1979): 35–47; Bernard Feld, "The Consequences of Nuclear War," *The Bulletin of the Atomic Scientists* 32, no. 6 (June 1976): 10–13; Louis René Beres, *Apocalypse: Nuclear Catastrophe in World Politics* (Chicago: Univerisity of Chicago Press, 1980), 315 pp.; *The Effects of Nuclear War*, a report by the U.S. Arms Control and Disarmament Agency, Washington, D.C., April 1979, 26 pp.; Bennett Ramberg, *Destruction of Nuclear Energy Facilities in War* (Lexington, Mass.: Lexington Books, D.C. Heath, 1980), 203 pp.; Michael E. Howard, "On Fighting a Nuclear War," *International Security* 5, no. 4 (Spring 1981): 3–17; Ruth Leger Sivard, *World Military and Social Expenditures 1980* (Leesburg, Va.: Arms Control Association et al., 1980), 35 pp.; Franklyn Griffiths and John C. Polanyi, eds., *The Dangers of Nuclear War* (Toronto: University of Toronto Press, 1979), 197 pp.; *U.S. Urban Population Vulnerability*, a report by the U.S. Arms Control and Disarmament Agency, Washington, D.C., August 1979, 50 pp.; Sidney D. Drell, "The Effect of Nuclear Weapons and Nuclear War on Civilians," a talk presented at the Symposium on the Effects of Nuclear War sponsored by the Physicians for Social Responsibility and the Council for a Livable World, Herbst Theater, San Francisco, November 17, 1980, 12 pp.; E.P. Thompson, "A Letter to America," *The Nation* 232, no. 3 (January 24, 1981): 68–93; Kevin N. Lewis, "Intermediate-Range Nuclear Weapons," *Scientific American* 243, no. 6. (December 1980): 63–73; George B. Kistiakowsky, *Can a Limited Nuclear War be Won? The Defense Monitor* 10, no. 2 (1981), 8 pp. (published by the Center for Defense Information, Washington, D.C.); *The Race to Nuclear War: Three Statements*, *The Defense Monitor* 9, no. 6 (1980), 8 pp.; *War without Winners*, *The Defense Monitor* 8, no. 2 (1979), 8 pp.; and the several conferences sponsored by Physicians for Social Responsibility on "The Medical Consequences of Nuclear Weapons and Nuclear War." A full report of the physicians' campaign to prevent nuclear war is contained in *The Bulletin of the Atomic Scientists* 37, no. 6 (June-July 1981).

2 Limited Nuclear War

Perhaps the most curious assumption of all accepted by current American nuclear strategy is that the USSR might decide to launch a limited first strike on the United States or its allies. Since America's developing counterforce capability is allegedly only for second-strike purposes, its rationale is necessarily based on the belief that a Soviet first strike might be limited. In the absence of such belief the commitment to damage-limiting retaliation would make no sense since this country's second-strike strategic forces would be expected to hit only empty silos.

But why would the Soviet leaders ever calculate that they have something to gain by launching a limited first strike? We have known for a long time that they do not share our view of controlled nuclear conflict and that there is no reason for them to believe our declared commitment to proportionate retaliation. Faced with great uncertainty about the nature of an American strategic response, Soviet leaders could not possibly make a rational decision to strike first in a limited mode. This is not to suggest that they would necessarily choose rationally to initiate total nuclear war with the United States, but only that once they had decided upon striking first they would be compelled to adopt a strategy of all-out assault rather than one of restraint.

These American views of nuclear strategy have their roots in the continuing search for a more credible policy of nuclear deterrence, one that would preserve a broad array of nuclear retaliatory options. Since such a policy is founded on the notion of a spectrum of deterrence, it led almost immediately to some tentative formulations of the idea of limited nuclear war. Ultimately many of these formulations found their way into the policies of the McNamara strategy of the 1960s and the successor strategies of James Schlesinger, Donald Rumsfeld, Harold Brown, and Caspar Weinberger.

Twenty years before Secretary Weinberger's five-year "defense-guidance" plan, McNamara, in a speech at the University of Michigan, described a strategy that went beyond the requirements of "minimum deterrence" and that included both counterforce and countervalue retaliatory options. Then as now the argument was advanced that credible nuclear deterrence mandates a strategy that allows for intermediate levels of military response, a second-strike counterforce strategy. Many elements of this strategy had been articulated several years earlier, by Henry Kissinger in his 1957 book, *Nuclear Weapons and Foreign Policy*. Confronting what he called "the basic challenge to United States strategy," Kissinger wrote:

> We cannot base all our plans on the assumption that war, if it comes, will inevitably be all-out. We must strive for a strategic doctrine which gives our diplomacy the greatest freedom of action and which addresses itself to the question of whether the nuclear age presents only risks or whether is does not also offer opportunities.[1]

The precise nature of Kissinger's preferred "strategic doctrine" here is preparation for limited nuclear war. While recognizing that the arguments against limited nuclear war are "persuasive," he insisted—in what must now be seen as a bellwether of current policy—that nuclear war need not be apocalyptic. Consequently, said the future secretary of state, "Limited nuclear war represents our most effective strategy against nuclear powers or against a major power which is capable of substituting manpower for technology."[2]

These ideas of a limited nuclear war—of a strategy of controlled annihilation—were also widely accepted by James Schlesinger during his tenure as secretary of defense. On March 4, 1974, Schlesinger testified before Congress in support of an American capability of reacting to a limited nuclear attack with selected counterforce strikes. According to his testimony such strikes could greatly reduce the chances for escalation into all-out strategic exchanges, thereby producing fewer civilian casualties.

Mr. Schlesinger's strategic doctrine, like that of his doctrinal forebears and successors, left many questions unanswered: What would be the probable effects of a limited nuclear war? What sorts of casualties might be expected in the wake of counterforce attacks against military targets envisioned in this plan for flexible response? Would the costs of a limited nuclear war really be limited, or would they be as overwhelming as the expected consequences of all-out, "spasm" nuclear conflict?

In his 1974 annual report as secretary of defense, Schlesinger remarked that nuclear attacks against American military installations might result in "relatively few civilian casualties." Subsequently, on September 11, 1974, the subcommittee on arms control of the Senate committee of foreign relations met with Schlesinger in executive session to consider the probable consequences of nuclear attacks against military installations in this country. During what transpired, the former defense secretary took a remarkably sanguine view, claiming that as few as 800,000 casualties could result from an attack on U.S. ICBM silos. This view was based on the assumptions of (1) a Soviet attack on all American Minuteman and Titan ICBMs with a 1-megaton warhead targeted on each silo and (2) extensive civil defense protection.

Since Schlesinger's conclusions generated a good deal of skepticism among several senators, the Office of Technology Assessment (OTA) of the U.S. Congress was asked to evaluate the Department of Defense (DoD) calculations. In response to this invitation, the OTA convened an ad hoc panel of experts, chaired by Jerome Wiesner, which returned with the following summary of conclusions:

> The panel members examined the results of the analyses of nuclear attacks which were given the Senate Foreign Relations Committee by the Department of Defense, and the assumptions which went into these analyses, in some detail. They concluded that the casualties calculated were substantially too low for the attacks in question as a result of a lack of attention to intermediate and long-term effects. They also concluded that the studies did not adequately reflect the large uncertainties inherent in any attempt to determine the civilian damage which might result from a nuclear attack.[3]

Even more significantly, perhaps, the panel could not determine from DoD testimony any consistent set of hypothetical Soviet objectives in the assumed nuclear strikes. While the panel acknowledged that the Soviets could detonate a small number of nuclear weapons over isolated areas in the United States without producing significant civilian damage, it could not understand how they might possibly benefit from such an attack. The panel's assessment, therefore, was explicitly detached from the presumption that its members felt the analyzed scenarios to be sensible or realistic.

Indeed, the panel on nuclear effects insisted that any analysis of proposed changes in American target strategy be conducted within a larger set of considerations affecting policy in this area. Such considerations, it believed, must include the extent to which new strategies could be executed without escalation to general nuclear war; the effect on deterrence of nuclear war; the degree to which such policy increases or decreases U.S. reliance on nuclear weapons; the extent to which it raises or lowers the threshold of nuclear first use; and the effect on the perception of U.S. allies about the credibility of the American commitment to their security.

Ultimately the Department of Defense completed new calculations showing that under certain conditions an attack upon U.S. ICBM silos could result in casualties of between 3 and 22 million, as opposed to the 800,000 to 6.7 million previously cited by Schlesinger.[4] Regrettably, however, the discussion of a larger set of considerations called for by the panel on nuclear effects has yet to take place. As in the case of its doctrinal antecedents, current U.S. strategic policy is premised on an inherently flawed assumption: the military reasonableness of a limited nuclear attack.

Even if such attacks hold out the promise of *relatively* low casualty levels, there is little reason to believe that anything short of an all-out nuclear assault would make military sense to the Soviets. According to Dr. Sidney Drell's testimony before the Senate subcommittee on arms control, in order to carry out a militarily effective attack against American ICBMs, one that would destroy about 800 of 1,054, or 80 percent, the Soviets would have to unleash an attack that would cause approximately 18.3 million

American fatalities. And even so extensive a counterforce assault would not be entirely disabling, since the remaining American ICBMs would still constitute a "healthy robust retaliatory force."[5]

What has been developing for many years in American strategic planning circles, therefore, is a counterforce doctrine that both understates the effects of limited nuclear war and ignores the primary fact that such a war makes no military sense. There is in fact no clear picture of what the USSR might hope to gain from the kinds of limited counterforce attacks that determine the direction of current American strategic policy. Indeed everything known about Soviet military strategy indicates that it has no place whatsoever for the idea of limited nuclear war. In the Soviet view all nuclear conflict would necessarily be total.

Once the nuclear firebreak has been crossed, it is most unlikely that conflict could remain limited. Ironically this point was hinted at by Henry Kissinger in 1965, when he wrote: "No one knows how governments or people will react to a nuclear explosion under conditions where both sides possess vast arsenals."[6] And it was understood by the four prominent authors of an article that appeared with much fanfare in the spring 1982 issue of *Foreign Affairs*: "It is time to recognize that no one has ever succeeded in advancing any persuasive reason to believe that any use of nuclear weapons, even on the smallest scale, could reliably be expected to remain limited."[7]

The credibility of the case against limited nuclear war was underscored in March 1982 by a five-day war game played by American command authorities. Code-named "Ivy League," the game represented the first time in 25 years that the United States command structures and communications systems that would be used in nuclear war were given a complete exercise. According to a report by the *Wall Street Journal*, the exercise began with assumptions of rising international tension and both the USSR and the United States mobilizing for war. After Soviet attacks on American forces overseas, war was declared, a U.S. ship was sunk in the North Atlantic, and U.S. troops overseas were attacked by troops using chemical warfare. The president then ordered a "low-level" nuclear retaliation and the war escalated to uncontrolled dimensions. After a 5,000-megaton missile attack on the United States, the game ended with the killing of the president (as a result of the blast) and with his successors completing the job of worldwide obliteration.[8]

While the prudent course would appear to assume that any onset of a nuclear exchange must be avoided lest it become total, current American strategic policy underscores counterforce targeting and its corollary recognition of limited nuclear war-fighting. Although it is clear that once a nuclear exchange has begun it would become impossible to verify yields, sizes, numbers, and types of nuclear weapons employed, current policy reaffirms the notion of limited exchanges conducted in deliberate and controlled fashion. A counterforce capability can serve only the nation that strikes first. Used in retaliation, counterforce-targeted warheads would hit only empty silos. Indeed, a second-strike counterforce strategy is simply a contradiction in terms.

We should not be surprised, therefore, when Soviet spokesmen continue to characterize America's nuclear strategy as a provocative move toward an eventual American first strike.[9] In their view this assessment is supported by this country's planned deployment of new medium-range missiles in Western Europe, a plan they say is designed to draw Soviet retaliation away from the United States in the aftermath of the American first strike. According to Vladimir Goncharov, a political news analyst for Tass, there is no doubt that this indeed is the American intention.[10]

The Soviet assessment of aggressive American designs is also supported, in their view, by this country's plan to place Soviet civilian and military leaders in particular jeopardy and by various overwhelming technological difficulties associated with counterforce doctrines of retaliation. While the essential rationale of a limited and controlled nuclear conflict requires the *preservation* of adversary leadership once a war has begun, America's current nuclear strategy is geared toward destruction of the Soviet ruling elite at the outset. Such a strategy can only contribute to unlimited, uncontrolled nuclear war. Indeed, in view of this country's current inability to support its countervailing strategy with advanced weapons systems, the provocative targeting of Soviet leaders actually increases the likelihood of a Soviet first strike in the near term.

The absence of appropriate supporting weapons systems for a second-strike counterforce strategy has now been widely reported. In a letter written in April 1979 to then Secretary of Defense Harold Brown, General Richard H. Ellis, commander-in-chief of the Strategic Air Command, indicated that U.S. strategic nuclear forces were incapable of carrying out a selective counterforce targeting strategy and would be in this handicapped position until 1986. As reported recently by Drew Middleton, little has happened since General Ellis's statement to suggest pertinent force improvements. According to Middleton:

> Surveying the Strategic Air Command's prospects of launching a [counterforce] attack after an initial Soviet strike, [General Ellis] estimated that the B-52s and ICBMs in his force would be left with fewer than 1500 warheads. He conceded that the American fleet of ballistic missile submarines would probably escape crippling damage during a surprise attack. But he stressed that there would not be sufficient surviving forces to launch an effective operation against Soviet missile silos and to fulfill other tasks "at a level much above the assured destruction of Soviet urban/industrial targets".[11]

Similar concerns about the plausibility of our counterforce doctrine of retaliation have been expressed by Colin Gray, one of the most ardent supporters of a countervailing American nuclear strategy. Writing in response to my article criticizing Presidential Directive 59 in *Parameters*, the journal of the U.S. Army War College, Gray observed: "So far as physical assets are concerned, PD 59 cannot be implemented with current forces and C^3I [command, control, communications, and intelligence] capabilities. Even if there were no reason to question the merit of the strategic vision in PD 59,. . . the United States is the better part of a decade away from a matching force posture."[12]

For the most part these reservations about the strategic force capabilities needed to support a second-strike counterforce strategy center on the alleged vulnerability of America's silo-housed ICBM force. To reduce such perceived vulnerability during the next few years, the United States may move toward launch-on-warning (sometimes called launch under confirmed attack) targeting policies.[13] While such policies might help to secure U.S. Titan, Minutemen, and silo-housed MX missiles against surprise attack if adequate information were immediately accessible to our national command authorities (the president, the secretary of defense, and their duly deputized alternates or successors), they would also portend an expanded risk of accidental nuclear war and Soviet preemption.

Launch-on-warning policies would also depend upon the successful functioning of the U.S. alert apparatus. Should this apparatus fail to function for any reason, including Soviet preemption, chances are that no decision to launch could be made or implemented in the few minutes available. At this time the USSR already has operational a high-energy laser weapon that may be capable of destroying U.S. satellites in low earth orbit. According to a recent report in *Aviation Week and Space Technology*, U.S. intelligence analysts believe that the Soviet high-energy laser weapon is capable of damaging subsystems and sensors on U.S. satellites at 100 kilometers, and that the Soviets are working on more powerful laser weapons that will be able to damage optical sensors on U.S. early warning and reconnaissance satellites at altitudes up to 40,000 kilometers.[14] Moreover, even if the Soviets were unable to jeopardize the American warning systems, it is virtually certain that their first strike would entirely disable this country's guidance and communications systems with killer satellites. Since an effective damage-limiting counterforce retaliation at Soviet hard targets (strategic forces and control centers that are protected to a significant extent against the effects of a nuclear attack) would require ultraprecise satellite guidance, this Soviet capability precludes such a retaliation.

Reservations about the strategic force capabilities needed to support a second-strike counterforce strategy also center on the alleged need for weapons engineered with a view to neutralize time-sensitive, hardened point targets (silos, submarine pens, nuclear storage sites, and command bunkers). However, the search for requisite combinations of accuracy, payload, yield, and responsiveness to create single-shot hard target kill capabilities is seriously misconceived, since it mistakenly presumes that a Soviet first strike would be executed with substantial forces held in reserve. And since such a search increases Soviet fears of an American first strike, it also heightens the probability of Soviet preemption.

Soviet fears of an American first strike might also be self-fulfilling. Such fears might occasion their own adoption of launch-on-warning strategies, expanding the risk not only of accidental nuclear war, but also of preemption by the United States. Once again the synergistic effects of America's current nuclear strategy are at variance with the objectives sought by that strategy. Rather than strengthen nuclear deterrence, the American search for a countervailing strategy will inevitably increase the likelihood of nuclear war with the USSR. The search will inevitably generate an escalatory cycle of move and countermove with complex interactive effects.

When the superpowers become engaged in the uncertain dynamics of escalation, they will find themselves in the precarious situation of trying to steer a steady course between the sheer rock of Scylla and the whirlpool of Charybdis. Should one side or the other back down out of fear, the retreat would probably be costly in terms of future global influence and power. Should both sides continue to exploit the presumed advantages of committal to warfare, the resulting escalation could well produce nuclear holocaust.

Herman Kahn once tried to identify some of the dangers that lurk in the hideously complex dynamics of escalation by likening these dynamics to the game of "chicken:"

> Both cars straddle the white line and drive toward each other at top speed. The first driver to lose his nerve and swerve into his own lane is "chicken"—an object of contempt and scorn—and he loses the game. The game is played among teenagers for prestige, for girls, for leadership of a gang, and for safety (i.e., to prevent other challenges and confrontations).[15]

Since the actual processes of escalation are much more complicated than this game, however, Kahn suggests that "chicken" would present a more accurate analogy if

> it were played with two cars starting an unknown distance apart, traveling toward each other at unknown speeds, and on roads with several forks so that the opposing sides are not certain that they are even on the same road. Both drivers should be giving and receiving threats and promises while they approach each other, and tearful mothers and stern fathers should be lining the sides of the roads urging, respectively, caution and manliness.[16]

The second metaphor is hardly more reassuring than the first. Whichever way the game is played, the prospect of collision is unaccaptably high. However much care is exercised, the fact that the game is being played by imperfect and vulnerable human beings underscores an inescapable truth: The process of superpower escalation is the start of a lethal partnership. Ultimately the partners and perhaps a substantial number of bystanders as well must suffer irreversible consequences.

But the game goes on. In the United States the national leaders continue to develop a nuclear strategy based on the prospect of limited nuclear war. Unaware that the interactive effects of such a strategy encourage brinksmanship, these ironically called "realists" can be counted upon to do their best to hasten the unthinkable.

It might be argued, of course, that the reasonableness of a second-strike counterforce strategy is *not* contingent on the assumption that a Soviet first strike would be limited. Such an argument would rest upon the understanding that the Soviets have a refiring and reconstitution capability with their missiles and that even an unlimited first strike would take place in several successive stages.[17] It follows from such an understanding that American counterforce-targeted warheads used in retaliation would not necessarily hit empty silos. They would also hit silos that might otherwise spawn weapons to enlarge the damage of the Soviet first strike.[18]

There are several problems with this argument. The most important one is that it is oriented entirely to issues of nuclear war-*fighting*. Accepting the likely prospect of a nuclear war (some, like Richard Pipes, speak of its near inevitability) and the probable failure of nuclear deterrence, it concerns itself (in conjunction with plans for multilayer ballistic missile defense, air defense, and civil defense) exclusively with damage limitation during a war. Although such concern may appear reasonable in principle, in fact it is misconceived. This is because very little of the United States would be left to protect after the first round of Soviet attacks had been absorbed (we do not even target submarine-launched ballistic missiles [SLBMs]) and because the countervailing strategy makes such attacks more likely in the first place by undermining stable deterrence.[19] In cost/benefit terms it should be clear that the benefits from damage limitation alleged to accrue to the United States from its countervailing strategy during a nuclear war are greatly outweighed by that strategy's deterrence-undermining costs.

Yet some analysts argue that the countervailing strategy actually supports stable deterrence. According to Colin Gray, for example, a vital connection exists between "likely net prowess in war and the quality of pre-war deterrent effect."[20] This view was also articulated by former Secretary of Defense Harold Brown in his speech at the U.S. Naval War College at Newport, Rhode Island, in August 1980. In these remarks, which represented a clarification of Presidential Directive 59, Brown stated:

> deterrence remains, as it has been historically, our fundamental strategic objective. But deterrence must restrain a far wider range of threats than just massive attacks on U.S. cities. We seek to deter any adversary from any course of action that could lead to general nuclear war. Our strategic forces must also deter nuclear attacks on smaller sets of targets in the U.S. or on U.S.military forces, and be a wall against nuclear coercion of, or attack on, our friends and allies. And strategic forces, in conjunction with theater nuclear forces, must contribute to deterrence of conventional aggression as well. . . . In our analysis and planning, we are necessarily giving greater attention to how a nuclear war would actually be fought by both sides if deterrence fails. There is no contradiction between this focus on how a war would be fought and what its results would be, *and* our purpose of insuring continued peace through mutual deterrence. Indeed, this focus helps us achieve deterrence and peace, by ensuring that our ability to retaliate is fully credible.[21]

These views suggest that successful deterrence of a Soviet first strike requires an American strategy to fight a nuclear war that would allow this country's forces to "prevail." But why should this be correct? The Soviet Union is no more likely to be deterred by an adversary that has announced its intention to dominate escalation processes during a nuclear war than by one that remains content with the capacity for assured destruction. Given their views about the implausibility of limited nuclear war, the Soviets already calculate on the basis of total nuclear effort by both sides. It follows that since the American search for a nuclear war-fighting capability heightens Soviet fears of American first-strike intentions, this search actually *degrades* this country's security. Moreover American strategic weapons that are counterforce-targeted to conform to nuclear war-fighting doctrines of deterrence will have significantly *reduced* deterrent effect since it is clear that their use in a second strike would produce substantially less damage to the USSR than would extensive countervalue attacks.

In the final analysis, nuclear weapons can serve the requirements of deterrence only where they threaten to destroy life and property. Since they are inappropriate tools for the military commander, these weapons make the idea of counterforce highly suspect. Ironic as it may seem, the only reasonably sane strategy for nuclear weapons is represented by the acronym MAD.

The strategic nuclear weapons in superpower arsenals now number approximately 16,500. In the absence of a new strategic arms control agreement, they will reach at least 26,000 by 1985. Is such growth in the number of strategic weapons needed to maintain an assured destruction capability?

Many of the most terrible consequences of atomic destruction can be found only in the less tangible regions of the human psyche. As revealed in the definitive scientific report on Hiroshima and Nagasaki, the victims were burdened not only with the well-known inventory of biological effects but also with an almost inconsolable hopelessness and anguish—what has been termed "keloid of the heart" and "leukemia of the spirit." According to the report, *Hiroshima and Nagasaki: The Physical, Medical and Social Effects of the Atomic Bombings*:

> The A-Bomb experience was brutalizing. In a sociopsychological survey of the households of 332 A-bomb victims and those of 268 nonvictims conducted in Kure City in October 1952, it was found that, among surviving victims who had been within 1 kilometer of the hypocenter at bombing time, the tendency was for children to abandon parents and for husbands to abandon their wives (mothers' attitudes toward children was different) and seek only their escape. Such behavior destroys one's trust in human relations and gives rise in time to "keloid of the spirit," and was in clear contrast to the behavior of nonvictims. The depth of such inner suffering can hardly be measured quantitatively on a universal scale.[22]

Notes

1. From p. 15 of Kissinger's *Nuclear Weapons and Foreign Policy* (Garden City, N.Y.: Doubleday, 1957).
2. Ibid., p. 166.
3. *Analyses of Effects of Limited Nuclear Warfare*, a report prepared for the Subcommittee on Arms Control, International Organizations, and Security Agreements of the Committee on Foreign Relations, U.S. Senate, September 1975, p. 4.
4. Opening Statement by Senator Case to Hearing before the Subcommittee on Arms Control, International Organizations, and Security Agreements of the Committee on Foreign Relations, United States Senate, on "Possible Effects on U.S. Society of Nuclear Attacks against U.S. Military Installations," September 18, 1975, p. 3.
5. Dr. Drell's testimony of September 18, 1975, ibid., p. 21.
6. Kissinger's introduction to *Problems of National Strategy*, a book of readings edited by him (New York: Praeger, 1965), p. 6.
7. McGeorge Bundy, George F. Kennan, Robert S. McNamara, and Gerard Smith, "Nuclear Weapons and the Atlantic Alliance," *Foreign Affairs* 60, No. 4 (Spring 1982):757.
8. "U.S. Reportedly Tried Practicing Doomsday War," *The Wall Street Journal*, March 26, 1982, p. 1. The White House and the game participants have remained publicly silent about the exercise, which reportedly involved more than 1,000 civilian and military personnel. In the exercise, the part of the president was allegedly played by William P. Rogers, former secretary of state, while former CIA Director Richard Helms is said to have played the vice-president.
9. See, for example, "Soviet Charges Reiterated," *The New York Times*, August 21, 1980, p. A8. In this connection, it should be understood

that Soviet images of the United States as a nuclear adversary have long been founded on the plausibility of an American first strike. For examples of such images, see V.D. Sokolovsky, ed., *Soviet Military Strategy*, 3rd ed., H.F. Scott (New York: Crane, Russak, 1968), pp 56–57; A. Grechko, "V.I. Lenin i stroitel'stvo sovetskikh vooruzhennykh sil," *Kommunist* 3 (February 1969):15–26; and William D. Jackson, "Soviet Images of the U.S. as Nuclear Adversary 1969–1979," *World Politics* 4 (July 1981): 614–38. Nonetheless, since late 1979 the Soviet leadership has expressed heightened alarm over the U.S. quest for strategic counterforce planning and theater nuclear force improvements.

10. See "Soviet Charges Reiterated."

11. Drew Middleton, "SAC Chief Is Critical of Carter's New Nuclear Plan," *The New York Times*, September 7, 1980, p. 19.

12. My article was "Presidential Directive 59: A Critical Assessment," *Parameters* 11, no. 1 (March 1981):19–28. The quotation is from p. 32 of Gray's article in the same issue, "Presidential Directive 59: Flawed but Useful." The same conclusion is reached by a recent report to the Congress by the comptroller general of the United States, *Countervailing Strategy Demands Revision of Strategic Force Acquisition Plans*, U.S. General Accounting Office, MASAD-81-35, August 5, 1981, 54 pp.

13. U.S. launch-under-attack policies appear to be taken very seriously by the Reagan administration. Earlier receptivity to such policies was announced by former Defense Secretary Brown: "The question is, would you launch land-based missiles before explosion of nuclear weapons on the United States? It is not our doctrine to do so—neither is it our doctrine that under no circumstances would we ever do so." From p. 68 of Brown, "Launch on Warning or Launch under Attack?" *Defense/Space Daily*, November 11, 1977, cited by John M. Collins in *U.S.–Soviet Military Balance: Concepts and Capabilities 1960–1980*, New York: McGraw-Hill, 1980), p. 129 n.

14. *Aviation Week and Space Technology* 112, 24, (June 16, 1980): 60–61.

15. Kahn, *On Escalation: Metaphors and Scenarios* (New York: Praeger, 1965), p. 10.

16. Ibid., p. 12.

17. See, for example, Secretary of Defense Weinberger's testimony to the Senate foreign relations committee concerning "Strategic Weapons Proposals," 97th Congress, First Session, on The Foreign Policy and Arms Control Implications of President Reagan's Strategic Weapons Proposals, November 3, 1981 (Washington, D.C.: 1981 U.S. Government Printing Office), p. 20.

18. For an example of this argument, see "Nuclear War and Europe," the Heritage Foundation, *National Security Record* 40 (December 1981):5. Heritage Foundation analysts disclose that sources within the Department

of Defense report a Soviet intensification of SS-18 rapid reload exercises. The danger of such exercises, according to these analysts, is that the "Soviet Union may be hoarding several thousand uncounted ICBMs in secret depots as their strategic reserve, rather than hold back any portion of their deployed forces." Yet these same analysts fail to ask the antecedent question: What conceivable mission might these reserves be designed to fulfill?

19. To be viable the countervailing strategy would not only have to display a high degree of assurance against ICBMs but would also require a superb antisubmarine capability and antibomber attack, all executed with what is called in military jargon "a most timely manner"—that is, virtually simultaneous with impact of the attacking weapons.

20. Quoted from p. 35 of Gray's "National Style in Strategy: The American Example," *International Security* 6, No. 2 (Fall 1981). In another article Gray says essentially the same thing: "Fortunately, there is every reason to believe that probable high proficiency in war-waging yields optimum deterrent effect." (p. 34 in "Presidential Directive 59: Flawed but Useful."

21. From p. 6 of the Remarks delivered at the Convocation Ceremonies for the 97th Naval War College Class, Newport, Rhode Island, August 20, 1980.

22. Report by the Committee for the Compilation of Materials on Damage Caused by the Atomic Bombings in Hiroshima and Nagasaki (New York: Basic Books, 1981), p. 14.

3 Improved Nuclear Deterrence

Current American nuclear strategy is also founded on the curious assumption that the USSR is more likely to be deterred by the threat of limited American counterforce reprisals than by the threat of overwhelming, total nuclear retaliation. Closely related to the assumption that a Soviet first strike might be limited, this assumption expands the American commitment to limited nuclear war as a plausible strategic option. Anticipating the prospect of limited levels of Soviet aggression, American nuclear strategy has operationalized an incremental policy of strategic response.

What this idea ignores is the stated Soviet unwillingness to play by American strategic rules. Since the USSR continues to threaten the United States with all-out nuclear war once American counterforce reprisals have been launched, the credibility of the American commitment to selective counterforce strikes must appear very doubtful. Once again the asymmetry in strategic doctrine between the superpowers on the plausibility of limited nuclear war impairs the credibility of America's nuclear strategy. There is now every reason to believe that the Soviet response to "limited" American counterstrikes would be just as overwhelming as it would be to a massive American countervalue strike. It follows that the alleged flexibility of our nuclear strategy is illusory, offering no advantages over a deterrence strategy of unlimited reprisals.

These flaws in American nuclear strategy are aggravated further by this country's own published doubts concerning controlled nuclear conflict. In the words of Harold Brown:

> In adopting and implementing this policy [the countervailing strategy] we have no more illusions than our predecessors that a nuclear war could be closely and surgically controlled. There are, of course, great uncertainties about what would happen if nuclear weapons were ever again used. These uncertainties, combined with the catastrophic results sure to follow from a maximum escalation of the exchange, are an essential element of deterrence.[1]

This argument is seriously confused. Rather than functioning as "an essential element of deterrence," the uncertainties to which Brown refers undermine the credibility of an American threat to employ a "measured" strategy of annihilation. And their effect is made all the more worrisome by virtue of their open expression. After all, Soviet perceptions of American strategic self-doubt can only reinforce their rejection of graduated nuclear conflict.

Similarly the uncertainties that would surround the response to any American use of nuclear weapons undermine this country's reliance on theater nuclear forces. In view of the enormously high probability of Soviet nuclear counterretaliation and the terrible destruction that would be visited upon allies "in order to save them," Soviet strategists cannot possibly accept claims of American willingness to use theater nuclear forces. Indeed in the aftermath of an overwhelming Soviet conventional assault against American allies, it could conceivably be more rational for this country's national command authority to bypass theater nuclear forces altogether, urging instead the immediate resort to a strategic strike.

The credibility of the American threat to use theater nuclear forces on behalf of allies has now been further eroded by the impending deployment of a new generation of medium-range ballistic missiles. Since these missiles, unlike existing theater forces, would pose a major threat to the Soviet homeland, their retaliatory capability carries a perceptibly higher risk of escalation than these existing forces. In fact, there is every reason to believe that these weapons would carry the same escalatory risk as strategic nuclear forces.

As in the case of other elements of this country's nuclear strategy, the NATO plan to deploy 572 advanced nuclear-armed missiles (108 Pershing II [PII] extended-range, battlefield-support ballistic missiles and 464 ground-launched cruise missiles [GLCMs]) would undermine deterrence and generate new Soviet incentives to preempt. As the first new U.S. land-based missiles in Europe in two decades that would have the capability of reaching targets in the USSR, they would offer no revolution in weapons design or operational role. Rather, they would seek to establish a "Euro-strategic" balance by neutralizing the threat of recently upgraded Russian intermediate-range nuclear weapons.

There is no deterrence role for the two U.S. missiles that could not be satisfied by existing or improved U.S. strategic systems, however. For one reason or another American thinking on the new intermediate-range forces is governed by the assumption that the Soviets are particularly sensitive to the warhead launching sites and that they would be less apt to engage in no-holds-barred nuclear war if an attack were launched from European bases. Regrettably, Soviet military doctrine has always regarded such fine distinctions as artificial and pointless.[2]

From the point of view of the USSR it would make little difference if an attack on its territory were from an American-based ICBM or from a European based PII or GLCM. Nevertheless American nuclear policy in this area is founded upon the myth that PII and GLCM deployments will create an "escalatory ladder that provides a variety of response options below the strategic level and helps to insure the linkage between lower response options and the strategic nuclear forces."[3] Such deployments are apt to produce not an "escalatory ladder" but *escalation*. According to the assessment of the U.S. Arms Control and Disarmament Agency:

> With the deployment of LRTNF [long-range theater nuclear force] systems in Europe, the Soviet Union may see itself confronted by mobile launchers capable of striking the USSR which, like Soviet theater systems capable of striking Western Europe, are not limited by existing arms limitation pacts. Further, the versatility of a mix of long-range theater nuclear systems could cause Soviet leaders to perceive themselves confronted with the potential at some future time for large-scale increase in the U.S. arsenal capable of striking the USSR. (Deleted) These perceptions could lead to expanded deployments of Soviet systems such as the SS-20 as a counter to any perceived strengthening of NATO's position vis-à-vis the Warsaw Pact.[4]

It was, perhaps, his understanding of these issues that led President Reagan, on November 18, 1981, to propose to reduce to zero all intermediate-range missile systems in the European theater. While the president's willingness to consider broad reductions in that theater represented an auspicious turn of events, it failed to include in the negotiations all U.S. medium-range nuclear weapons now deployed in Europe or assigned to NATO defense as well as the British and French nuclear arsenals. To offer any real chance of success, the IRBM negotiations must encompass the whole problem of European security. In this connection the prescriptions for a successful negotiating strategy were summarized by the American Committee on East-West Accord in a letter to the president on November 23, 1981. According to the committee, U.S. negotiating strategy should be based upon the following major principles:

1. priority consideration to restraining those weapons and those other aspects of the present arms race that make nuclear war more likely;
2. a specific and mutual renunciation of the concept of limited nuclear war;
3. a balanced reduction of armaments in such a manner as to maintain the concept and the fact of stable mutual deterrence;
4. a definition of medium-range theater nuclear weapons that includes all land, sea, and air-based weapons directed at the European area, specifically including U.S. and Soviet submarine-launched missiles, U.S. and Soviet aircraft capable of carrying nuclear weapons, and French and British nuclear forces;
5. recognition of the reality that a meaningful agreement on nuclear restraint and reduction cannot be concluded at the theater level alone but must also encompass intercontinental systems.

President Reagan's proposal called for dismantling of Soviet missiles with 1,130 warheads in exchange for cancellation of deployment of 572 Western cruise and Pershing II missiles. Full acceptance of this proposal would still leave the West with 562 medium-range theater nuclear weapons and the USSR with 57 medium-range SLBMs (submarine-launched ballistic missiles). It would also leave both sides in full possession of their present numbers of medium-range dual-capable (nuclear and conventional) aircraft.

Table 3–1
Medium-Range Theater Nuclear Missiles

Forces Encompassed by Reagan Proposal				
Land-based	*Soviet Missiles*	*Warheads*	*West*	
SS–20	250	750	Future cruise missiles	464
SS–5	40	40	Future Pershing II missiles	108
SS–4	340	340	Total	572
Total	630	1130		

Forces Not Included in Reagan Proposal			
	Soviet	*West*	
Submarine-based	57	SLBM Poseidon NATO	400 approx.
		UK Polaris	64
		French Polaris	80
			544 SLBMs
All medium-range nuclear-capable aircraft[a]		All medium-range nuclear-capable aircraft[a]	
		French IRBMs	18
		Western medium-range theater nuclear missiles	562

[a] Including those that also have a conventional capability.

Source: International Institute for Strategic Studies, *Military Balance 1981–82.*
Reprinted with permission from the American Committee on East/West Accord.

A similarly incorrect rationale surrounds the Reagan administration decision to proceed with full production of neutron weapons. While enhanced-radiation weapons would not constitute a threat to the Soviet homeland and while they would reduce damage, in comparison to existing tactical nuclear weapons, to friendly forces, civilians, and structures,[5] these miniature thermonuclear warheads would not enhance the credibility of this country's nuclear commitment to NATO. Such weapons would still represent a crossing of the critical "firebreak" between conventional and nuclear weapons. Hence in view of current Soviet policy to respond to any such crossing with unlimited retaliation, the use of the neutron bomb would carry an intolerably high risk of escalation to strategic nuclear war. In the words of Arthur S. Collins, Jr., a retired general whose last field assignment was as deputy commander-in-chief of the U.S. army in Europe:

> NATO use of neutron weapons . . . is going to draw a Soviet response with tactical nuclear weapons. . . . The asymmetry between Soviet nuclear weapons and the neutron bomb would be so great that the larger and less accurate Soviet weapons would be devastating to NATO forces using the small weapons.[6]

Whether the first nuclear weapons used between NATO and the Warsaw Pact were neutron bombs or tactical weapons, escalation to unlimited nuclear war would be very likely. This reality would obtain since any nuclear exchange would lead each side to press ahead with its entire arsenal. To do otherwise amidst the momentum of military operations, fear, anger, and uncertainty would be decidedly irrational. It is most likely his understanding of this fact that led President Carter, on April 7, 1978, to defer production of enhanced radiation weapons. It is the Reagan administration's misunderstanding of this fact that occasioned its decision in August 1981 to go ahead with production and stockpiling of the neutron bomb.

Even demonstrations of automatic reaction for alliance guarantees of nuclear retaliation cannot ensure the perception of willingness to retaliate. No matter how high a value the United States might place on "protection" of various allies (the term "protection" is somewhat ironic here, since execution of the nuclear retaliatory threat would most likely hasten the destruction of the ally to be protected), it can never be as high as the value that it places upon its own security. No matter how often or how vehemently the United States claims that an attack on our NATO allies would be tantamount to an attack on the United States itself, the claim is apt to be viewed as incredible. Hence no level of commitment by rational decisionmakers that involves a high probability of nuclear counterretaliation will be seen as irrevocable. Although the use of tactical nuclear weapons may not involve any greater destruction than the use of massive conventional firepower, the truly critical threshold or firebreak exists between conventional and nuclear weapons (including enhanced-radiation weapons) rather than between different forms of nuclear weapons. This is true because of the clear and verifiable distinction between nuclear and nonnuclear weapons, and because of the symbolic and psychological implications that accompany nuclear combat in any form. Nuclear weapons *are* different because they are widely *believed* to be different. It is now altogether likely that tactical nuclear retaliation (or retaliation with the neutron bomb) would be perceived as the beginning of a genuine no-holds-barred situation.

President Kennedy certainly understood this when he stated that "inevitably the use of small nuclear armaments will lead to larger and larger nuclear armaments on both sides, until the worldwide holocaust has begun."[7] This view is supported by *The Defense Monitor*, a publication of the highly regarded Center for Defense Information:

> Once the nuclear threshold has been broken it is highly likely that the nuclear exchanges would escalate. Radio, radar, and other communications would be disrupted or cut. The pressures to destroy the adversary's nuclear force before they land a killing blow would lead to preemptive attacks. In the confusion, subtle peacetime distinctions between lower level tactical nuclear war and higher level tactical nuclear war, and all-out

> spasm nuclear war would vanish. Once the threshold is crossed from conventional warfare to nuclear warfare, the clearest "firebreak" on the path to complete nuclear holocaust will have been crossed.[8]

Moreover, according to the sponsors of the First Conference on Nuclear War in Europe, which took place in Groningen, the Netherlands, in April 1981:

> NATO plans for many years have provided for an initial strike against the Warsaw Pact with nuclear weapons, and it would be only prudent military planning for the Soviet Union to retain a similar option.
>
> Once nuclear weapons have been exploded, there is no assurance their use can be controlled or stopped. No one knows the sequence of events which will follow the explosion of tens or hundreds or thousands of nuclear weapons. Up until the present, only one nuclear weapon has ever been fired at one time. Communications are certain to be disrupted for hours and it will be difficult, if not impossible, for either side to control its own forces.
>
> If any of the parties in the conflict wished to opt out it would be difficult to communicate with all of the four nuclear nations who maintain control over their own nuclear weapons. It takes only one nation to start a nuclear war in Europe, but it requires agreement of four nations to stop it. This may be impossible in view of the chaos which exploding nuclear weapons will bring. . . . U.S. military war plans for Europe and NATO war plans for Europe cover only the first few days of fighting. Attempts to "war game" hypothetical wars involving nuclear weapons have always failed because there is no comparable body of data to make valid predictions beyond the first few days.
> . . . it is instructive to note that the explosive power carried in just one NATO Polaris submarine exceeds the total explosive forces of all weapons fired in World War II, including the two atomic bombs exploded by the U.S. over Japan.[9]

In spite of this argument American NATO policy continues to emphasize the special role of theater nuclear forces as a deterrent to conventional as well as theater nuclear attacks. What is most peculiar about this emphasis is that it is coupled with the understanding that operational Soviet military doctrine does not subscribe to a strategy of graduated nuclear response and that the limited use of nuclear weapons is fraught with the danger of escalation. With such an understanding it is difficult to believe that the United States would actually be willing to make good on its theater nuclear commitments to NATO allies.

This difficulty is underscored by the effects that theater nuclear forces would have on the countries being protected. A recent study by the Center for Defense Information reveals that the use of only 10 percent of the roughly 7,000 tactical nuclear weapons maintained by the United States in Europe would destroy the entire area where these exchanges took place.[10] This situation would not be altered by deployment of the neutron bomb, since the expected Warsaw Pact counterretaliation would be devastating and unlimited.

In an examination of the consequences of nuclear war in Europe undertaken by the participants in the First Conference on Nuclear War in Europe, Henry W. Kendall, professor of physics at Massachusetts Institute of Technology, led the conferees through the probable data, concluding, as far as theater warfare is concerned, that with existing inventories the USSR easily "could kill nearly all the persons in the urban centers of Western Europe and subject those areas to near total destruction. Indeed, one might say the attack runs out of victims and targets."

> There is not inconsiderable chance that nuclear war in Europe would be accompanied by large-scale nuclear conflict between the Soviet Union and the United States of America, perhaps including China. If this were so, wholly new kinds of acute damage could be done to the global environment and to the global biosphere. Following such a general nuclear war, there would then arise the strong possibility that mankind, and indeed all life, could no longer continue as it always has. The specific problems of the European survivors would dissolve into the much larger calamity facing everyone.[11]

Philip Sonntag, researcher at the Wissenschaftszentrum Berlin, analyzed the predictable effects of limited war (no missiles of intercontinental range) on West Germany. He estimated that in a countervalue strike (a strike directed at population centers and industry), two-thirds of the industrial capacity would be destroyed along with other devastation. In a counterforce attack (one directed at military installations), the firing back and forth would virtually destroy the country.

> The emphasis on counterforce options comes out of the drive by military interests to have an attainable technical goal in order to further the establishment and self-preservation of military tasks and skills within the society. It is counter-productive because technical progress continuously produces new, dangerous weapons in an attempt to gain military superiority, without taking into account that carrying out such a "defense" in fact destroys what it should preserve. Yet we only have a chance to avoid nuclear war if political priority prevails.[12]

Patricia J. Lindop of St. Bartholomew's Hospital in London, after analysis of the radiation effects to be expected from nuclear war in Europe, pronounced nuclear weapons militarily useless because their radioactive fallout would be "unconstrained . . . unlimited by national or political boundaries, nor even by military objective."

> Indeed, it was the unpredictability of radioactive fallout patterns which early in the development of nuclear weapons made the active military leaders realize that nuclear weapons were unusable in tactical warfare,

> whether in the desert or in Europe. Emphasis was therefore given to their strategic effect as deterrents. The principle of deterrence was held until the lessons of the weapons tests of the early '50s were forgotten, and a new generation began to believe in the concept of a limited or tactical nuclear war. . . . [The] essence of military action is planning and prediction of weapons use and effects; and protection of military personnel and equipment. Radioactive fallout makes this impossible. [For example,] with the high density of population in Western Europe, a single nuclear weapons attack on a reactor, say in West Germany, would render uninhabitable for a long time a large part of its area and of the surrounding countries. . .[13]
>
> But all this does not make the situation hopeless. In arms control negotiations it is often remarked that only those weapons which have been shown or known to be militarily useless have been successfully banned by treaty.[14]

Lindop's last point, about "military useless" weapons, has particular relevance to the neutron bomb. In addition to its very high potential for escalation to all-out nuclear war, the neutron bomb has no real military value since its tactical potential against Soviet tanks is decidedly inferior to existing fission weapons. In view of the fact that nuclear radiation kills slowly, a Soviet tank crew that would suffer a lethal dose from enhanced-radiation weapons might still be able to fight for a day or more. To be confident that he has really put a Soviet tank out of action, a NATO field commander could not possibly rely on the destructive effects of radiation; he would need tangible evidence of visible damage from the *blast* of an explosive.[15]

With the neutron bomb American strategic planners argue that they could kill the Warsaw Pact soldiers inside their tanks rather than destroying the tanks themselves. Yet in the very unlikely event of a Russian-led Warsaw Pact blitzkrieg across the nothern plains of West Germany, the high neutron flux generated by enhanced radiation would prove distinctly inferior to existing tactical weapons. While current NATO doctrine stipulates that "immediate transient incapacitation," which requires only 2,500 to 3,500 rads (the measure of radiation dose) should be sufficient to neutralize invading forces, this calculation is fraught with uncertainty. A dose of 3,000 rads incapacitates within 5 minutes, but the victim may recover partially within 30 minutes. Although he remains a doomed man until his horrible death four to six days later, he may still be able to fight on for some time.[16]

The argument for the neutron bomb has been cast in terms of the illusory spectrum of deterrence that would offer the president a set of flexible options in crisis situations. It is now being widely suggested in certain quarters that this flexibility can be made more effective by emphasizing the American capacity and willingness for nuclear war-fighting.[17] Codified in Secretary of Defense Weinberger's five-year plan, current U.S. strategic objectives include preparations for nuclear counterattacks against the USSR "over a protracted period."[18] And of course such preparations are based on the premise that the USSR is getting ready to fight and win a nuclear war. Ironically this premise is at odds with another major assumption of current American nuclear strategy—that the Soviets might launch a limited nuclear first-strike and subsequently cooperate in a limited nuclear war with the United States.

In the Soviet view a nuclear war could occur only if the "imperialists" launched a sudden first strike or if a regional conflict were to escalate out of control.[19] Should the overriding goal of deterrence meet with failure, however, their doctrinal and policy imperatives call for the realization of several major objectives concerning damage limitation and steps toward recovery. Although there is no evidence that these objectives entail the search for "victory," they preclude any sort of limited nuclear response. According to John M. Collins, author of the most comprehensive modern study of the U.S.–Soviet military balance, the Soviet response to any American first use of nuclear weapons would not be restricted to "punitive reprisals that serve the State poorly." Therefore, says Collins:

> The Politburo assigns a low priority to sophisticated concepts for limited nuclear war, if known aspects of Soviet doctrine are any indication. There is doubt, for example, that diplomatic ballets and finely-tuned bargaining would reduce dangers. Esoteric signals, such as symbolic, exemplary, and talionic (tit-for-tat) strikes, might well be missed or misunderstood in the heat of the nuclear battle. . . . The Soviets therefore may well abandon most constraints once the threshold of nuclear combat has been crossed and, abiding by the adage "never send a boy to do a man's job," employ whatever power is needed to defeat opponents expeditiously.[20]

Leaving aside these contradictory assumptions of current American nuclear strategy, the alleged linkage between capacity for nuclear war-fighting and credible deterrence is inherently ill-founded. Contrary to the opinions of various strategic mythmakers who believe that in confronting an adversary who appears to believe that it is possible to fight and win a nuclear war,[21] the United States must display a parallel belief, there is no reason to believe that the USSR can be deterred only by the prospect of "losing" a nuclear war. In assessing the anticipated effects of alternative courses of action, Soviet leaders would have no reason to calculate that the absorption of *any* American nuclear reprisal would fall within "acceptable" levels (unless, of course, they were convinced that an American first strike were imminent).

As with certain other aspects of current American nuclear strategy, the emphasis on creating a nuclear war-fighting potential is entirely counterproductive to this country's security. This is the case because such an emphasis goes beyond the reasonable requirements of an assured destruction capability to a provocative demonstration of first-strike intentions. Whether or not such intentions are genuine (and I seriously doubt that they are), all that matters are Soviet *perceptions*. The logic of deterrence requires a demonstrated willingness and capacity to deliver an unacceptably damaging retaliation after absorbing a first strike, but where such demonstrations are supplanted by certain forms of counterforce posturing, incentives are created for a rational adversary to preempt.

This point was made with characteristically succinct elegance by Paul C. Warnke in testimony before the Senate foreign relations committee:

> To meet our deterrent purpose, what we need are nuclear weapons that are the most survivable and the least provocative. By that I mean that our strategic nuclear weapons systems must be known to be able to ride out a preemptive first strike and retain the capability to inflict devastating damage in retaliation. At the same time, they should not be weapons that pose a serious threat to the deterrent forces on the other side. If they do so, the other side may panic at a time of major international crisis and conclude that it must "use them or lose them."[22]

This testimony identifies the central flaw in current American nuclear strategy. Virtually all of the essential elements of this strategy occasion doubts among Soviet leaders about this country's alleged rejection of a nuclear first strike. Rather than reinforce American security by projecting the image of survivable and assuredly destructive nuclear forces that we are prepared to use in retaliation, this strategy undermines American security by fostering the impression of first-strike inclinations. By encouraging a climate of strategic interaction in which the USSR must exist in a continual and increasing expectation of imminent attack, the United States compels its adversary to take steps to strike first itself. Naturally these steps are perceived as aggressive in turn, and in "reaction" to apparent Soviet designs an unstoppable cycle of move and countermove is initiated. The net effect of course is insecurity for all concerned.

Current American nuclear strategy therefore enlarges rather than reduces the likelihood of nuclear war with the Soviet Union. Even if the Soviets would prefer a condition of protracted enmity with the United States to a superpower nuclear war, the expectation of an American first strike may encourage them to strike first themselves. This is the case because they may believe that certain damage-limiting benefits would accrue to the country that strikes first. Of course they would anticipate extraordinary levels of destruction for themselves and would prefer nonwar to relative strategic advantage *if they had the choice*. But faced with a situation they perceive to omit peace as an option, they would be compelled to choose preemption as the rational course.

It follows from this analysis that American nuclear strategy is seriously flawed in creating the impression of preferring relative victory to nonwar. Even if this impression is erroneous, all that matters is that it is perceived as genuine in Soviet strategic calculations. Regrettably, everything about current American nuclear strategy encourages such a perception. To reverse such a dangerous perception while there is still time, this strategy must seek to communicate a different set of expectations to the USSR, one that clarifies this country's distinct preference for nonwar over any conceivable outcome of nuclear conflict. With such clarification the USSR would be less inclined to calculate that rationality requires preemption, and the United States would be in a position to implement parallel processes of deescalation.[23]

To give meaning to such clarification, the United States should attend immediately to various offensive qualities of the MX missile. Not only will the announced MX basing mode fail to reduce the widely alleged vulnerability of the ICBM leg of the triad, perceptions of the MX's preemptive attack qualities will detract from stable deterrence. Designed to deliver its enormously destructive load within 100 meters of target, the MX seeks to fulfill an American search for a high probability of a single-shot kill against "hard targets" (missile silos, submarine pens, nuclear storage sites, and command bunkers).

According to the testimony of Admiral Eugene J. Carroll, Jr. (Ret.) before the Senate foreign relations committee:

> On the vulnerability issue, the Reagan Administration has painted itself into a corner. With its decision to go forward with MX in fixed silos it has conceded that for the time being the vulnerability problem either does not exist or is insoluble. They have not adequately answered why placing them in what they view as vulnerable silos does anything to correct the situation. Proceeding with the MX missile in fixed silos can only be interpreted by the Soviets that the U.S. intends them to be first strike weapons.[24]

Shortly after Admiral Carroll's remarks, the same point was made by Ethel Taylor, national coordinator of Women's Strike for Peace:

> The junking of the MX shell game reveals, I think, what the MX really is. We were told it was supposed to have made our land-based missiles invulnerable to attack, in other words, a defensive weapon. The abandonment of the railway system strips away that facade, I think, and raises a question whether or not the MX is a highly accurate multiple warhead missile for which there is really no other purpose than a first strike.[25]

Since it has been proposed to "protect" the MX with ballistic missile defense (BMD) systems, the destabilizing effects of that weapons system might be further enlarged. This is the case because such deployment would generate a parallel Soviet deployment, which would in turn generate a mutual search for new counterforce missile capabilities. Taken together, such deployments would heighten each side's fear of a first strike by the other, a condition that would also remove any lingering prospects for the negotiation of a strategic arms reduction agreement.[26]

Yet supporters of the MX counterforce targeting qualities argue that there is no reason to make such Soviet targets safe from U.S. ICBMs when comparable targets in this country are at risk from Soviet ICBMs. But this argument is based entirely on the confusion of survivability and targeting objectives, and it substitutes monkey-see-monkey-do logic for a well-reasoned deescalation of strategic competition. Indeed, considered together with America's failure to ratify SALT II; its continuing failure to seriously seek strategic arms control with the Soviet Union, its continuing reliance on a policy of nuclear first use; its program to modernize long-range theater nuclear forces; and its renewed commitments to ballistic missile defense and civil defense; the MX potential to place Soviet strategic forces in jeopardy naturally provides the Soviet Union with a greater incentive to strike first.

The destabilizing aspects of the MX are paralleled by other American strategic force developments. The Trident II missile and warhead programs are designed to provide U.S. countersilo capabilities that could put a significant portion of Soviet fixed ICBMs at risk. Although Trident II's potential hard-target kill capabilities are intended to provide a hedge against catastrophic failure of the other legs of the triad, it will almost certainly stimulate the Soviets to increase the number of attacking reentry vehicles (RVs). Similarly the MK-12A RV is now being acquired to replace the MK-12 RV on 300 of the 550 Minuteman III missiles currently deployed. Since the essential rationale of this planned deployment is to expand the ICBM force's counterforce capability, the MK-12A RV will also heighten Soviet fears of American preemption. According to an assessment offered by the U.S. Arms Control and Disarmament Agency:

> The MK-12A RV was designed to be employed against the total spectrum of targets but increasingly has been planned for employment against a growing Soviet hardened target system, where its combination of yield and accuracy could be used to military advantage. Although the MM III in its current configuration is effective to some degree against hard targets, improved accuracies which may accrue as a result of the guidance improvement program and the higher yield of the MK-12A (W78) warhead would increase this capability.[27]

Moreover, what is our purpose in placing Soviet military and civilian leaders in particular jeopardy? Is it, as one strategic analyst suggested recently, "to destroy the ability of the Soviet leadership to continue to exercise political control over its domestic and 'colonial' territory—either by killing the leadership itself, making it impossible for the leadership to communicate with its subordinates, or destroying the means . . . by which the leadership's orders are carried out?"[28] If this *is* the purpose, then it is clearly contrary to the essential rationale of a countervailing nuclear strategy: that is, preserving the prospects for limited, controlled nuclear conflict.

But what about the Soviets? Are not *their* current deployments and capabilities provocative and destabilizing? Are not *they* continuing to strive for nuclear superiority that is oriented toward a "win the war" potential and that is augmented by a far-reaching civil defense effort? Have they not been developing precision guidance for their heavy MIRVed ICBMs, the SS-18 and SS-19, with a view to threatening the survival of U.S. ICBM forces?

The evidence is hardly encouraging. The steady growth of Soviet military power has fostered legitimate questions over Soviet strategic objectives. It may even be true, as concluded earlier, that Moscow's buildup stems from patently aggressive designs. But it is *not* true, even if our "worst case" assumptions are correct, that American security is best served by acting in an equally provocative or more provocative manner.

In developing a long-term defense program vis-à-vis the USSR, the U.S. government should be guided exclusively by a careful comparison of the costs and benefits of alternative courses of action. Such a comparison must take careful note of expected Soviet reactions to American military developments and of the long-range *cumulative effects* of these developments. It will make precious little sense, for example, to increase funding substantially for BMD research and development since the Soviets can be expected to offset the ICBM survivability benefits with a refined offensive strategic capability.

Maintaining the survivability of the U.S. strategic triad (ICBMs, SLBMs, and manned bombers equipped with missiles and gravity weapons) must continue to be an overriding goal of this country's defense posture.[29] But it is altogether clear that this goal will not be served by the planned MX system and its associated counterforce weapons systems. Again, Soviet countermoves must be anticipated. And it is likely that the expanding search for hard-target kill capacity will do more to undermine deterrence than to provide safety. The fact that the Soviets are already engaged in such a search in no way suggests the rationality of American imitation.

A similar argument must be made concerning renewed American interest in civil defense. In what is likely to become the reduction to absurdity of American imitativeness, the Reagan administration has begun to call for funding to implement a "crisis relocation plan" (CRP). Were it to be subjected to careful scrutiny in terms of expected costs and benefits, CRP would be revealed as immensely impractical and needlessly provocative. Rather than strengthening deterrence by demonstrating this country's war preparedness (a demonstration that the USSR seems no longer to need), plans for crisis relocation would underscore Soviet fears of an American first strike. Indeed, even if it were assumed that large-scale U.S. civilian evacuation plans were workable and that a government-directed civilian exodus several days before a nuclear war would not degenerate into chaos, a Soviet nuclear attack could still doom virtually every American.

According to Irwin Redlener, a doctor who has studied CRP for Physicians for Social Responsibility, such civil defense calculations by American authorities are "based on little hard data." Ignoring the many important differences that exist between a city being evacuated in the face of a hurricane and one being flattened by a nuclear bomb, says Redlener, CRP rests on highly questionable analogies rather than upon well-reasoned analysis. Furthermore,

> CRP makes the basic assumption that a warning time of one week is essential to effect any reasonable degree of evacuation and protection. This discounts any possibility of a surprise attack. The elimination of a presumptive attack scenario makes little sense even to traditional military planners.
>
> CRP requires the evacuated families to shovel piles of dirt around the buildings to which they are assigned in order to make them "radiation safe"—but doesn't speak to how this might be accomplished during the winter months in a northern climate. Even in the national "model" areas (such as Plattsburgh, New York) where it has been rather fully developed, there is no real provision for the management of hospitalized patients in the target sites or for the redirection of essential services such as food supply.
>
> Finally, evacuating U.S. counterforce and other target sites carries the distinct possibility of provoking the war it claims it will protect us from. How would an adversary interpret such an evacuation? Could this mean the U.S. was preparing to deploy its first strike weapons? If so, would not the Soviets feel the need to strike first? Such considerations are logical, lethal, and apparently disregarded by current civil defense planners.[30]

Another authoritative assessment of the relocation option has been undertaken in *Nuclear Weapons*, a recent report of the secretary general of the United Nations. This assessment is remarkable for its deliberate understatement.

> Evacuation of population from areas expected to come under attack has to be planned very carefully in advance. Apart from transportation and housing of evacuees, this planning must include at least short-term provisions for the relocated population. Information and instructions to the general public would have to be issued in advance. Even if instructions were available, however, the execution of an evacuation would probably be accompanied by confusion and panic. Large-scale evacuation is, therefore, in most cases, no attractive option.
>
> To start an evacuation too early would mean an unnecessary disruption of everyday activities; to start too late would worsen the prospects for those evacuated, as their vulnerability would be highest during the transfer phase. The very fact that an evacuation had started might even precipitate the attack, and there is also the possibility of targeting the relocated population. These constraints are valid in any type of war, but in a nuclear war they would be more severe. In addition, there is the particular problem of radioactive fallout, as available radiation shielding can generally be expected to be inferior in rural areas. Furthermore, the location of serious fallout areas cannot be predicted in advance.[31]

Notes

1. Brown, *Annual Report of the Department of Defense for FY 1981* (Washington, D.C.: U.S. Government Printing Office), p. 67.

2. For a sound, critical analysis of the planned NATO deployment of intermediate-range nuclear weapons, see Kevin N. Lewis, "Intermediate Range Nuclear Weapons," *Scientific American* 243, no. 6 (December 1980): 63–73.

3. See the section on "Long-Range Theater Nuclear Missile Systems and the Sea-Launched Cruise Missile," in *Fiscal Year 1982 Arms Control Impact Statements*, Submitted to the Congress by the President (Washington, D.C.: U.S. Government Printing Office), (February 1981), pp. 200–38, which contains statements prepared by the U.S. Arms Control and Disarmament Agency (ACDA).

4. Ibid., p. 230. The ACDA report also points out that a hazard of planned deployments includes a negative impact on the prospects for arms control.

5. These weapons would produce the bulk of their damage by a flood of neutrons rather than through heat or concussive force. Following are some terms used in measuring radiation doses:

> *Rad*. The standard unit of radiation absorbed, a term that supersedes the roentgen as the unit of dosage. The rad is the unit for measuring the amount of radiation to which the whole body, as opposed to a single organ, is exposed. A millirad is one-thousandth of a rad. Doses of a few millirads are now considered safe, but there is still debate over the thresholds between a safe and a hazardous dose.
>
> *Roentgen*. A measure of the quantity of X-ray or gamma radiation in the air.
>
> *Rem*. For "roentgen equivalent, man," it is the biological effect produced by one roentgen of X ray. "Millirem" is the term used to describe the measuring of absorption of radiation by human beings. The average American is exposed to 100 to 200 millirems of radiation per year, including radiation from X rays to cosmic rays. A normal chest X ray exposes a person to 20 to 30 millirems.

6. Arthur S. Collins, Jr., "The Enhanced Radiation Warhead: A Military Perspective," *Arms Control Today* 8, no. 6 (June 1978): 5.

7. John F. Kennedy, *The Strategy of Peace* (New York: Harper & Row, 1960), p. 185.

8. *The Defense Monitor* 4, no. 2 (February 1975): 3.

9. *Nuclear War in Europe: A Report*, sponsored by the Center for Defense Information, Washington, D.C., and the Polemological Institute, State University of Groningen, The Netherlands, 1981, p. 8.

10. *The Defense Monitor* p. 3.

11. *Nuclear War in Europe*, p. 28.

12. Ibid., p. 29.

13. It must be remembered, several speakers pointed out, that Western Europe has numerous power reactors. Their destruction, which can be accomplished by conventional bombs, would release enormous radioactivity.

14. Ibid., p. 29.

15. Herbert Scoville, Jr., "The Neutron Bomb Makes Politics, Not War," *The New York Times*, August 26, 1981, p. 25. Dr. Scoville is president of the Arms Control Association and a former high official in the Central Intelligence Agency.

16. Fred M. Kaplan, "Enhanced-Radiation Weapons," *Scientific American* 238, no. 5 (May 1978): 48. The destructive effects of the neutron bomb are due to the ionizing effects of neutrons colliding with protons inside living cells. Ionization breaks down chromosomes, swells cell nuclei, increases the viscosity of cell fluid, enhances cell-membrane permeability, and destroys cells of all kinds, particularly those of the central nervous system. Exposure to ionizing radiation also delays or destroys the process of mitosis, a long-term genetic effect that inhibits normal cell replacement.

17. See, for example, the writings of Gray and Payne, Sloss, and Pipes cited in Chapter 1 as well as the recently articulated policies of Eugene Rostow at ACDA and Caspar Weinberger at the Defense Department.

18. See Richard Halloran, "New Atom War Strategy Confirmed," *The New York Times*, June 4, 1982, p. 7.

19. *The Philosophical Heritage of V.I. Lenin and Problems of Contemporary War*, edited by Maj. Gen. A.S. Milovidov, translated for U.S. Air Force, Soviet Military Thought Series, no. 5 (Washington, D.C.: U.S. Government Printing Office, 1974), p. 100.

20. John M. Collins, *U.S.–Soviet Military Balance: Concepts and Capabilities 1960–1980* (New York: McGraw-Hill, 1980), p. 118. The author, a senior specialist in national defense at the Library of Congress, has served in strategic and combat intelligence, in joint contingency planning, and on the faculty of the National War College, where he was director of military strategic studies and first chief of the strategic research group.

21. See the previously cited reactions of Colin Gray and Leon Sloss to my article on PD 59 in *Parameters*.

22. *Strategic Weapons Proposals*, Hearings before the Committee on Foreign Relations, United States Senate, 97th Congress, First Session, on "The Foreign Policy and Arms Control Implications of President Reagan's Strategic Weapons Proposals," November 9, 1981 (Washington, D.C.: U.S. Government Printing Office) p. 109.

23. In this connection special attention should be given to Charles E. Osgood's very promising GRIT (graduated and reciprocated initiatives in tension-reduction) strategy. For information on this strategy, see Osgood's "Psycho-Social Dynamics and the Prospects for Mankind," presented to the Peace Science Society (International) in 1977 and to a UN colloquium in 1978; and his article "The GRIT Strategy," *The Bulletin of the Atomic Scientists* 36, no. 5 (May 1980): 58–60.

24. Testimony before the committee, November 9, 1981, p. 139.

25. Ibid., p. 143.

26. It should also be noted that the prospects for reliable ballistic missile defense are extremely remote. In recent research at Massachusetts Institute of Technology and other universities, workshop participants concluded that even orbiting lasers would stand little chance of defending against a missile attack; the technological obstacles are insurmountable and such weapons would be vulnerable to simple countermeasures. According to Kosta Tsipis, a leading student of laser weapons, "We have concluded that lasers have little or no chance of succeeding as practical, cost-effective defensive weapons." See Tsipis's "Laser Weapons," *Scientific American* 254, no. 6 (December 1981): 52. In this respect current research into ballistic missile defense possibilities has reaffirmed the earlier conclusions of Andrei Sakharov, who was critically involved with development of the Soviet H-bomb. See Andrei D. Sakharov, *Progress, Coexistence and Intellectual Freedom* (New York: W.W. Norton, 1968), p. 35. See also Herbert F. York, *Race to Oblivion, A Participant's View of the Arms Race* (New York: Simon and Schuster, 1970), ch. 10, "The Defense Delusion."

27. *Fiscal Year 1982 Arms Control Impact Statements*, February 1981, p. 3.

28. Jeffrey T. Richelson, "The Dilemmas of Counterpower Targeting," *Comparative Strategy* 2, no. 3 (1980): 226–27.

29. It has never really been made clear that even the existing American ICBM force is genuinely vulnerable to a Soviet first strike: the Soviets could not calculate that such a strike might be undertaken in a fashion that would preclude overwhelmingly destructive American retaliation. Arguments against the so-called window of vulnerability were submitted to the Townes commission during summer 1981 by Edward Anderson, a professor at the University of Minnesota, and by Christopher Paine of the Federation of American Scientists. These papers, which demonstrate convincingly that the USSR would not be able to knock out U.S. ICBM forces (much less the other two legs of the American triad) are inserted into the records of *Hearings* before the Senate committee on foreign relations, "Strategic Weapons Proposals," November 1981. Also included in the record is an article by Michael McGwire discussing the operational limitations of deploying nuclear cruise missiles on attack submarines. Moreover, according to a recent report by the Council on Economic Priorities, "Minuteman is not

nearly as vulnerable as claimed by the Pentagon." Indeed, adds the report, "even a vulnerable Minuteman would leave the Soviet Union faced with a massive retaliatory capability." (See Tom Wicker, "Rethinking the MX," *The New York Times*, August 25, 1981, p. 27.) This view is corroborated by an editorial in the conservative military journal *Strategic Review*. Questioning the accuracy of Soviet missiles in light of such imponderables as weather, gravity, magnetic fields, planned interference, technical reliability timing and fratricide, the journal's military editor, Arthur G.B. Metcalf, concludes: "No refutation has been offered to the finding that Minuteman 'vulnerability' is without foundation" (Wicker, ibid.). The same conclusion is reached by Andrew and Alexander Cockburn, "The Myth of Missile Accuracy," *The New York Review of Books*, November 20, 1980, pp. 40–43; reprinted in *Parameters* 11, no. 2 (June 1981): 83–89. For more on the serious liabilities of the MX, see Herbert Scoville, Jr.'s, important book, *MX: Prescription for Disaster* (Cambridge, Mass.: MIT Press, 1981), and Center for Defense Information, "MX: The Weapon Nobody Wants," *The Defense Monitor* 10, no. 6 (1981). In considering the costs and benefits of striking first, the Soviets would also have to consider the possibility of a U.S. "launch under attack" response, something far more feasible for the American solid-fuel Minuteman force than for the liquid-fuel Soviet ICBMs.

30. From the, *PSR Newsletter*, April 1980 and summer 1981. Copyright © by Physicians for Social Responsibility. For more information on nuclear weapons and war, write: PSR, 639 Massachusetts Avenue, Cambridge, Mass. 02139.

31. See *Nuclear Weapons*, Report of the Secretary-General (Brookline, Mass.: Autumn Press, 1980), p. 102, published with the authorization and cooperation of the United Nations. The book presents the complete report entitled *General and Complete Disarmament: Comprehensive Study on Nuclear Weapons: Report of the Secretary-General*, which was presented to the UN General Assembly in fall 1980. It was prepared pursuant to Resolution 33/91 D of December 16, 1978, whereby the general assembly requested the secretary-general with the assistance of qualified experts to carry out a comprehensive study on nuclear weapons.

4 Survival

The third major assumption of current American nuclear strategy is that survival is possible in a superpower nuclear war. Closely related to the other flawed assumptions concerning limited nuclear war and improved nuclear deterrence, this assumption makes nuclear war more likely by contributing to the impression that such a war might be tolerably sustained. Contrary to recent findings of the medical and scientific communities, this assumption rejects the informed understanding that a nuclear war would be uniquely and unavoidably catastrophic.

Although this assumption was recently detached from the idea that a nuclear war might be distinctly winnable (Secretary Weinberger's June 3 1982, speech at the U.S. Army War College), it remains tied to the idea that U.S. forces might "prevail" in a protracted nuclear war with the Soviet Union. It follows that while the Reagan administration may no longer accept the notion of victory in the sense of an improved outcome, it continues to believe in the advantages that would accrue from the capacity to dominate escalation. Hence its semantic changes notwithstanding, current U.S. nuclear strategy still reflects the ideas advanced by Colin Gray and Keith Payne, members of the professional staff at the Hudson Institute:

> Recognition that war at any level can be won or lost, and that the distinction between winning and losing would not be trivial, is essential for intelligent defense planning. . . . If American nuclear power is to support U.S. foreign policy objectives, the United States must possess the ability to wage nuclear war rationally.[1]

Nuclear war, we are told, can be waged "rationally." Here the United States is urged to achieve strategic superiority—the "ability to wage a nuclear war at any level of violence with a reasonable prospect of defeating the Soviet Union and of recovering sufficiently to insure a satisfactory postwar world order." And in a burst of uninformed optimism, the two strategic planners tell us: "A combination of counterforce offensive targeting, civil defense, and ballistic missile and air defense should hold U.S. casualties down to a level compatible with national survival and recovery."[2]

Yet from what we already know about probable effects of such targeting and defense measures, this level must have been defined at a very high figure. Presumably "national survival and recovery" could take place without the benefit of any significant number of living human beings. Even if an

American counterforce retaliation were enormously effective (a very optimistic assumption), there would be little left to protect after absorption of the Soviet first strike. Indeed, even if a nuclear war were to begin with an American first strike (that would undoubtedly be called a "first use"), there is every reason to believe that the Soviet retaliation would thoroughly decimate American society.

Leaving aside the widely understood limitations of defense against nuclear attack, there is considerable evidence that estimates of counterforce lethality have been grossly exaggerated in U.S. strategic planning circles. Neither side could exploit its counterforce strategy to prevent its own destruction. And this is the case whether the counterforce strategy were exploited for a first strike or for "damage limiting" retaliation.

Nevertheless it would be reasonable to conclude that in the long run fixed land-based missiles could become increasingly vulnerable to a MIRV (multiple independently targetable reentry vehicle—a missile payload comprising two or more warheads that can engage separate targets) attack. In such a case, however, the "benefits" of a counterforce strategy (assuming parallel breakthroughs in antisubmarine warfare) would accrue only to the side that strikes first. Used in retaliation, the damage to be expected of weapons assigned to hard targets would be insignificant; that is, it would not preclude overwhelming destruction. It follows that the continued counterforce arms race is exceptionally destabilizing, providing incentives not for peace but for preemption.[3]

The American effort in the expansion of counterforce operations is proceeding with breakneck speed. Fueled by the most ambitious buildup of nuclear weaponry in U.S. history, this effort will result in 17,000 new nuclear weapons over the next decade. Moreover through advances in propulsion, guidance, and engineering, our ICBMs and other nuclear delivery systems are being readied to destroy Soviet missile silos and command bunkers.

This drive for superiority and for presumed capacity to fight and win a nuclear war is supported by a number of specific technological objectives. In addition to the well-known planned deployment of the hard-target killing MX, 300 Minuteman III missiles are being retrofitted with the Mark 12A reentry vehicle. Each of these 900 RVs (three weapons per missile) will have twice the accuracy and twice the explosive power of the weapons on other Minuteman IIIs. This will give each retrofitted Minuteman III ten times the lethality of a Minuteman II.

The administration has also upgraded progress on maneuverable reentry vehicles (MARV—a ballistic-missile reentry vehicle equipped with its own navigation and control systems capable of adjusting its trajectory during reentry into the atmosphere). Ostensibly designed as a hedge against any future Soviet ABM threat, an advanced version of this weapon system (AMARV) will have nearly 100 percent accuracy. Such accuracy, a function of its ability to correct its trajectory during the reentry and terminal phases of flight, could exacerbate Soviet fears of an American first strike. These fears would be all the more reasonable when one considers parallel American developments in the size of MX and Minuteman III forces and in the development of advanced ballistic reentry vehicles (ABRV). Similarly, the now stepped-up production of a larger, more accurate Trident II (D-5) missile will certainly alarm the Soviets, as will some current and projected improvements in command, control, communications, and intelligence (C^3I) programs.[4]

Why should such improvements in American C^3I capabilities alarm the Soviets? After all, a credible deterrence posture requires an extensive global network that gives the White House, the Pentagon, and Strategic Air Command (SAC) headquarters the ability to communicate with all elements of U.S. strategic forces. Since C^3I systems are designed to warn command authorities of imminent nuclear attack and send out appropriate orders, should this country continue to upgrade its satellites, computers, underground antenna grids, special aircraft, ground-based radars, space-based sensors and soon even lasers?

The problem lies in the overall objective of the planned C^3I improvements. This is the creation of a C^3I network that can continue to operate *throughout the course of a nuclear war.* Steps are already underway to make out C^3I systems more survivable, jam resistant, and secure so that our nuclear forces could conduct a protracted nuclear war. While it is essential to maintain the credibility of our nuclear retaliatory threat, C^3I improvement measures are apt to delude our leaders into believing that a nuclear war is controllable, fightable, and survivable. It follows that these measures also serve to reinforce developing Soviet fears of an American first strike.

Expressing the fear that codified current American nuclear strategy has now moved beyond the legitimate requirements of nuclear deterrence, Paul Warnke offered the following testimony to the U.S. Senate foreign relations committee in 1981:

> I have one underlying and hard-to-document discomfort about the [strategic weapons] program. This derives from the occasional hints of a hope of developing forces to fit a strategy of nuclear war fighting rather than nuclear war prevention. Like Presidential Directive 59, developed and announced by the Carter Administration in the summer of 1980, there are implicit suggestions that we might be able to fight, survive and win a limited, protracted strategic nuclear war. To some extent, the proposals to strengthen communications, command and control may be motivated by this myth. To some extent, the investment in more strategic defense, particularly a civil defense program, may have this as an underlying assumption. To some extent, the emphasis on the greater accuracy of the MX and D-5 [Trident II] missiles may reflect this objective. I think it is important that the Senate determine whether the new strategic program, or any

> parts of it, are intended to implement a new and immensely dangerous strategy. Neither we nor the Soviet Union can win a nuclear war.[5]

Testifying later on the same day before the Senate foreign relations committee, Rear Admiral Eugene J. Carroll (Ret.) offered statements that support Mr. Warnke's apprehensions. According to Admiral Carroll, associate director of the Center for Defense Information in Washington, D.C., the Reagan administration's search for a nuclear war-fighting capability will heighten the risk of nuclear war.[6]

In considering the delusions of administration strategists who suggest that survival is possible, one must ask whether those responsible have even taken the trouble to consider the available scientific literature on nuclear war. If they *have* considered this literature, how can they explain their own sweeping dissent? Perhaps they should take a moment to pause and reflect upon an open letter to former President Carter and Chairman Brezhnev from a respected organization, Physicians for Social Responsibility:

> As physicians, scientists, and concerned citizens, alarmed by an international political climate that increasingly presents nuclear war as a "rational" possibility, we are impelled to renew a warning, based on medical and scientific analyses, that:
>
> 1. Nuclear war, even a "limited" one, would result in death, injury and disease on a scale that has no precedent in the history of human existence;
>
> 2. Medical "disaster planning" for a nuclear war is meaningless. There is no possible effective medical response. Most hospitals would be destroyed, most medical personnel dead or injured, most supplies unavailable. Most "survivors" would die;
>
> 3. There is no effective civil defense. The blast, thermal and radiation effects would kill even those in shelters, and the fallout would reach those who had been evacuated;
>
> 4. Recovery from nuclear war would be impossible. The economic, ecologic, and social fabric on which human life depends would be destroyed in the U.S., the U.S.S.R., and much of the rest of the world;
>
> 5. In sum, there can be no winners in a nuclear war. Worldwide fallout would contaminate much of the globe for generations and atmospheric effects would severely damage all living things.[7]

If this assessment of the consequences of nuclear war should appear exaggerated, consider the dangers associated with only one of the many health threats in the postattack environment—the threat posed by dead human beings. According to the distinguished physician, Herbert L. Abrams:

> The health threat created by millions of post-attack corpses is a serious one. In many areas radiation levels will be so high that corpses will remain untouched for weeks on end. With transportation destroyed, survivors weakened, and a multiplicity of post-shelter reconstruction tasks to be performed, corpse disposal will be remarkably complicated. *In order to bury the dead, an area 5.7 times as large as the city of Seattle would be required for the cemetery.* [Emphasis added.][8]

For anyone who has known or studied the effects of the atomic bombings of Hiroshima and Nagasaki, it is clear that a superpower nuclear war would bring not only death, but incoherence. In the words of Robert Jay Lifton:

> The ultimate threat posed by nuclear weapons is not only death, but meaninglessness: an unknown death by an unimaginable weapon. War with such weapons is no longer heroic; death from such weapons is without valor.[9]

Such meaninglessness would be accentuated by the impairment of symbolic immortality, a process by which human beings ordinarily feel that they can "live on" through their posterity. Since the occasion of superpower nuclear war would represent an assault on the very idea of posterity for millions of people, death would take place without rebirth, and the continuity of life would give way to authentic feelings of disintegration, separation, and stasis.

Such ideas were explored a number of years ago by Lewis Mumford:

> Facile calculations of how many people might physically survive for a limited period in deep underground shelters give no hint of the psychological traumas awaiting those emerging into a blasted landscape whose skies would still rain poison, whose unblasted surfaces would be covered with putrefying organisms, and whose food, in places where it could still be grown, would likewise be befouled with cancer-producing susbstances; while if, as is likely, in the total psychosis brought on by such a nuclear encounter, the military strategists resorted to still more desperate modes of extermination, by anthrax and botulism, even the well-protected "elite," governmental and military, might find, like Hitler in his terminal air raid shelter, that suicide would be preferable to facing such survivors as had escaped instant incineration.[10]

Recently, Howard Hiatt, dean of the Harvard School of Public Health, testified before the Senate subcommittee on health and scientific research on the consequences of a nuclear attack on Washington, D.C.[11] In view of the graphic and authoritative nature of this testimony, the entire statement is reproduced as follows:

A Nuclear Attack on Washington

Recent talk by public figures about winning or even surviving a nuclear war must reflect a widespread failure to appreciate a medical reality: any nuclear war would inevitably cause death, disease and suffering of epidemic proportions and effective medical interventions on any realistic scale would be impossible. This reality, in turn, leads to the same conclusion public health specialists have reached for such contemporary epidemics as those of lung cancer and heart disease: prevention is essential for effective control.

Little is said about the catastrophe of a nuclear attack, perhaps because it is horrible to contemplate. Surely, little is said about medical intervention because so little that is hopeful can be said. And yet, our very silence permits or encourages the nuclear arms race to continue, making almost inevitable, either by design or by chance, what could be the last epidemic our civilization will know.

Much can be said, however. Two sources of information are available. The first are descriptions of the medical effects of the Hiroshima and Nagasaki bombs. The second are several recent and authoritative theoretical projections of the medical effects of bombing American—or Soviet—cities toward which Soviet— or American— nuclear weapons are now aimed.

The Hiroshima bomb, the explosive power of which was equivalent to 20,000 tons of TNT, is estimated to have killed 100,000 out of a total population of 245,000, 25% directly burned by the bomb, 50% from other injuries, and 20% as a result of radiation effects. It destroyed two-thirds of the 90,000 buildings within the city limits. Perhaps even more devastating than the statistics are the descriptions of individual victims. Consider this picture presented by John Hersey in his book, *Hiroshima*:

"There were about 20 men . . . all in exactly the same nightmarish state: their faces were wholly burned, their eye sockets were hollow, the fluid from their melted eyes had run down their cheeks. . . . their mouths were swollen, pus-covered wounds, which they could not bear to stretch enough to admit the spout of the teapot . . . "

A recent study, prepared by the U.S. Arms Control and Disarmament Agency, postulated a one-megaton bomb attack on Washington, D.C., and it is upon that source that these remarks are based.

The scenario which I shall present is, you must realize, conservative. While the 1-million ton bomb involved in the attack is far more destructive than the Hiroshima and Nagasaki bombs, so, too, is it far less destructive than the largest contemporary weapons. And this hypothetical attack involves the detonation of only a single weapon, whereas contemporary military planning and technological capabilities make it far more likely that several weapons will be used in each attack.

Washington's trial by nuclear attack begins with the detonation of a 1-megaton air burst bomb above the White House. The area of total destruction, the circle within which even the most heavily reinforced concrete structures do not survive, has a radius of 1.5 miles. That circle includes within it virtually every major monument, the heart of the city's subway system, and indeed, this very room. And within this circle, too, almost all of the population is killed.

At a distance of 3 miles from the White House, past the Arlington National Cemetery, concrete buildings are destroyed. The heat from the explosion and the spontaneous ignition of clothing cause third-degree flash burns over much of the body, killing most people in this area.

More than 4 miles from the center, brick and wood frame buildings are destroyed and fires caused by the intense heat are fanned by 160-miles per hour winds.

In a circle extending to Takoma Park, Hyattsville, and Suitland, brick and wood frame buildings sustain heavy damage. The heat exceeds 12 calories per square centimeter and all individuals with exposed skin suffer severe third-degree burns.

Nearly 9 miles from the center, in McLean, Alexandria, and Bethesda, including the Walter Reed and Bethesda Naval Hospitals, brick and wood frame structures sustain moderate damage.

Miles beyond this last ring, people suffer second-degree burns on all exposed skin and additional burns from flammable clothing and environmental materials. Retinal burns resulting from looking at the fireball cause blindness. As high winds spread the fires caused by the initial blast and thermal radiation, the number of casualties grows.

If we assume a population for the metropolitan area of 2.5 million, one-quarter of the inhabitants—more than 600,000—are killed. Even more—800,000—are injured. Many of these survivors are badly burned, blinded, and otherwise seriously wounded. Many are disoriented. These are the short-term effects; the problem of radiation sickness, including intractable nausea, vomiting, bleeding, hair loss, severe infection, and often death, will grow in the days and weeks ahead and fallout from the bomb will spread well beyond the area of impact.

The population is devastated; many survivors are in need of immediate medical care, food, shelter, clothing and water. The communities in which they have lived have, in many cases, virtually ceased to exist as physical entities—and as social entities as well. Government is barely existent. The transportation system, including many roads, has been destroyed. Remaining food, water, and medical supplies are dangerously inadequate.

And what of the medical response to such a disaster? In Hiroshima, 65 of the city's 150 doctors were killed in the bombing and most of the survivors were wounded. Some 10,000 wounded made their way to Hiroshima's 600-bed Red Cross Hospital. There, only 6 doctors and 10 nurses were able to help them. . . .

And what of Washington? Taking as our base a figure of 6,000 physicians in the metropolitan area and extrapolating from the casualties suffered by the general population, we may project that 1,500 doctors will be killed immediately and some 2,000 will be seriously injured. Thus 2,500 surviving physicians will be responsible for the care of 800,000 patients with grave wounds. It will take five 16-hour workdays for each of these patients to be visited once—for 15 minutes.

In fact, it is likely that many fewer physicians will survive, for they are concentrated, during working hours, in an area close to the center of the blast. But whether the postattack physician-to-patient ratio is 1:300 or 1:1,000, where will treatment take place?

The bomb will reduce the number of hospital beds, within the District alone, by more than 60%, and the amount of medical equipment and supplies are similarly inadequate. Can the seriously injured be treated at George Washington University Hospital? It no longer exists. Georgetown University Hospital? It, too, has been destroyed. In ruins, as well, are Howard University Hospital, D.C. General, Capitol Hospital, and several others. The geographic distribution of surviving medical facilities will be another problem, some requiring physicians to enter more highly radioactive areas, and thus expose themselves to greater personal danger, in order to treat the injured.

With a decimated professional community, physical facilities largely in ruins, and a complete disruption of communications, the task of treating the wounded will be hopeless. . . .

While the Massachusetts General Hospital has 15 beds for the acute care of such burn victims, "just to keep one such patient alive taxes us," Dr. John Burke, the director of the Burn Unit, told me.

Indeed, keeping the one patient alive is a triumph of modern medicine. But it requires the extraordinary resources of one of the world's major medical centers. No amount of preparation could provide the human and physical resources required for the care of even a few such patients hospitalized simultaneously in any city of the nation. Yet one must assume that at least tens of thousands of such casualties would result in every metropolitan center hit by a nuclear weapon.

This is but one reason that it is futile to suggest a meaningful rapid medical response to the overwhelming health problems that would follow a nuclear attack. Further, only the most limited medical measures can be visualized to deal with the burden of cancer and genetic defects that would afflict survivors and future generations. With respect to temporary evacuation, radioactivity would make the blast area uninhabitable for months. Most of the area's water supply, sanitation resources and transporation and industrial capacity would be destroyed.

The preparation of these remarks was for me as stressful as their contemplation must be to you. What purpose, I wondered initially, to describe such almost unthinkable conditions. But the conditions are not unthinkable; rather they are infrequently thought about. Among the painful results of the silence are the continuing proliferation of nuclear weapons and the failure to reject out-of-hand nuclear war as a "viable option" in the management of world problems.

I am grateful, Mr. Chairman, that you have undertaken to break the silence on this issue. There is, of course, no reason to consider the consequences of nuclear war in strictly medical terms. But if we do so, we must pay heed to the inescapable lesson of contemporary medicine: where treatment of a given disease is ineffective or where costs are insupportable, attention must be given to prevention. Both conditions apply to the effects of nuclear war—treatment programs would be virtually useless and the costs would be staggering. Can any stronger arguments be marshalled for a preventive strategy?

But prevention of any epidemic requires an effective prescription. The development of a prescription that will both prevent nuclear war and safeguard our security is a challenge that confronts all of us, and particularly our political leaders. Is there any other challenge that is more urgent or more important to all Americans and all people everywhere?[12]

Such expert testimony reflects a vitally important and growing phenomenon in the struggle to highlight the intolerable consequences of nuclear war—the expanding consciousness and involvement of the American medical community. As early as 1962 a series of articles in the *New England Journal of Medicine* outlined for the first time the probable medical and public health consequences of a "limited" nuclear strike against a metropolitan area. These articles estimated that the blast, fire storms, and acute ionizing radiation from detonation of only two nuclear weapons would kill 1,052,000 people of the Greater Boston population of 3 million. Of those expected to survive the immediate explosion, approximately 1 million would die from the injuries received. And of Boston's 6,560 physicians (1950 census figures) 4,850 were expected to be killed, 1,070 to be injured, while only 640 would remain uninjured.[13]

More recent assessments by American physicians indicate that these early conclusions were enormously conservative.[14] The earlier conclusions excluded natural consequences that would be overwhelming: long-term climatic changes, degradation of the stratospheric ozone layer, radioisotope contamination of food chains, and crop failures resulting from alterations in insect ecology. They also did not consider the possibility of blast-induced rupture of radioactive-waste storage containers and the release into the environment of plutonium and other toxic radioactive isotopes with half-lives measured in thousands of years.[15]

Fortunately a number of physicians have continued to face the gorgon's head of nuclear war with unaverted gaze. Recognizing that there can be no more meaningful therapeutic service than the prevention of nuclear war, these physicians have spearheaded a worldwide movement that seeks to counter the most dangerous form of denial ever to confront our species—the denial of an all-destructive nuclear apocalypse.[16] Although such denial may offer certain anxiety-reducing benefits, it also functions to prevent life-sustaining and system-transforming responses. Hence in both the medical and social scientific sense the benefits are outweighed by the costs.

It is heartening that a concerned group such as Physicians for Social Responsibility has seen its membership grow from 1,300 to 20,000 during 1982. Even more important perhaps, the pillars of the American medical establishment—the medical schools and societies—are getting more and more involved with the problem of nuclear war. In spring term 1982 at the Harvard Medical School, for example, "The Health Aspects of Nuclear War" was offered as a new elective course for students.[17] Moreover, other medical schools are taking similar action while a growing number of articles on the results of a nuclear war are appearing in major medical journals.

An article in the November 1981 issue of *The New England Journal of Medicine* generated a great deal of public attention to the problem of nuclear war.[18] Reflecting the world of the 1980s, the authors, Herbert Abrams and William E. Von Kaenel, assume a 6,559-megaton attack on the United States (the so-called CRP-2B model used by the Federal Emergency Management Agency in civil defense planning). Hence in terms of yield it represents 524,720 Hiroshima bombs.[19] As for the targets of the attack they are assumed, in order of priority, to include the following: military installations, military supporting industrial, transport, and logistic facilities; other basic industries and facilities that contribute to the maintenance of the economy; and population concentrations of 50,000 or greater.

What are the expected consequences of such an attack? According to the authors, 40 percent of the population would be killed at once and another 24 percent would die during the shelter period. Only about 28 percent of the population would survive unscathed.[20]

What sort of world would the survivors confront? Going beyond the already well-known recitation of the effects of burns, blast, and radiation, Abrams and Von Kaenel identify infection and the spread of communicable disease as the principal threat in the intermediate term. In this connection specific attention is given to the infection-susceptibility factors associated with radiation, trauma, and burn casualties, malnutrition and starvation, dehydration, exposure, hardship, and lowered natural resistance to disease. Factors affecting the spread of disease are identified as shelter conditions, sanitation, insects, corpses, and animals. The expected effect of burgeoning insect populations is especially stark and sobering:

> Insects are generally more resistant to radiation than are human beings. This fact, along with the prevalence of corpses, waste and untreated sewage, the depletion of birds, and the destruction of insecticide stocks and production, will engender a huge increase in insect growth. Mosquitoes would multiply rapidly after an attack . . . The fly population would explode . . . Most domestic animals and wild creatures would be killed. Trillions of flies would breed in the dead bodies. Uncontrolled growth in the insect population . . . may sharply limit the capacity to control such diseases as typhus, malaria, dengue fever and encephalitis.[21]

And what sorts of health measures might be arrayed against potential epidemics in the postattack environment? According to the authors the picture is grim. Because a large percentage of physicians practice in large cities, fatalities among doctors and other medical care providers might reach 80 percent. Abrams and Von Kaenel estimate that each of the surviving physicians would have to treat 177 trauma and burn victims, not to mention at least as many suffering from injuries, radiation sickness, and illness due to the epidemics that would no doubt ensue.[22]

Such medical testimony should be considered together with the systematically gathered insights of a 1975 study entitled *Long-Term Worldwide Effects of Multiple Nuclear-Weapons Detonations*. This report, prepared by a special committee of the National Research Council, National Academy of Sciences, was undertaken in response to a request by Fred C. Iklé, a former director of the U.S. Arms Control and Disarmament Agency and currently an assistant secretary of defense. Its point of departure, according to Philip Handler, president of the National Academy of Sciences (NAS), is

> a horrendous calamity: a hypothetical exchange involving the detonation of many nuclear weapons. In the worst case considered, about one half of all nuclear weapons in current strategic arsenals, viz., 500 to 1000 weapons of yield 10 to 20 megatons each and 4000 to 5000 lesser (sic!) weapons with yields of 1 or 2 megatons each, i.e., a total of 10^4 megatons (10,000,000,000 tons) of TNT-equivalent are exchanged among the participants. No report can portray the enormity, the utter horror which must befall the targeted areas and adjoining territories. Nor does this report so attempt.[23]

What the report does portray are the long-term, worldwide effects following the exchange of 10,000 megatons of explosive power in the northern hemisphere, in a plausible mix of low- and high-yield weapons, and at a variety of altitudes of detonation. Acknowledging the "unimaginable holocaust" that would occur in the primarily afflicted nations, the report confines its attention to possible long-term effects on more distant populations and ecosystems, with special reference to the atmosphere and climate, natural terrestrial ecosystems, agriculture and animal husbandry, the aquatic environment, and both somatic and genetic effects upon humans.[24]

Although the report concludes that the biosphere and the species *Homo sapiens* would survive the hypothetical strategic exchange,[25] it recognizes that humankind's civilization might not survive such catastrophic insult. This conclusion has nothing to do with the probable social, political, or economic consequences of the hypothesized nuclear exchange, consequences characterized by the report's writers as "entirely unpredictable" effects of "worldwide terror" and deliberately not discussed. Instead the topic is the interrelated physical and biological aspects of this calamity. The following possibilities are predicted: temperature changes in either direction and of different magnitudes; major global climatic changes; contamination of foods by radionuclides; worldwide disease epidemics in crops and domesticated animals because of ionizing radiation; shortening of the length of growing seasons in certain areas; irreversible injury to sensitive aquatic species; long term carcinogenesis due to inhalation of plutonium particles; some radiation-induced developmental anomalies in persons *in utero* at the time of detonations; increase in skin cancer incidence of about 10 percent, which could increase by as much as a factor of 3 if the ozone depletion were to rise from 50 to 70 percent; severe sunburn in temperate zones and snow blindness in northern regions in the short term; and an increased incidence of genetic disease that would not be limited to the offspring of the exposed generation but would extend over many generations.

Of course accurate prediction of the worldwide consequences of all-out nuclear war between the superpowers is fraught with uncertainty. With this in mind the participants in the six separate committees who produced the NAS report caution their readers about the limitations of the data upon which their conclusions rest. It would be prudent, therefore, to recognize that the devastating effects expected by the NAS scholars might be only the tip of the iceberg and that other perhaps even more significant effects would accompany the hypothesized exchange. The plausibility of such recognition is underscored by the fact that the magnitude of the war postulated in *Long-Term Worldwide Effects of Multiple Nuclear Weapons Detonations* may be much too low. Were the superpowers to exchange between 50,000 and 100,000 megatons of nuclear explosives, rather than the 10,000 megatons assumed by the report, global climatological changes would imperil the very survival of humankind.

The predicted effects of nuclear war between the superpowers are uncertain for a second reason, interactions between individual effects. While a good deal is already known about the separate effects of a nuclear exchange, we cannot rule out that the interactions among these effects would be utterly unexpected and deadly. To understand fully the effects of a nuclear war between the superpowers, we must go beyond the usual separate examinations of the consequences of blast, nuclear radiation, and thermal radiation to a full consideration of possible synergy among these consequences.

In March 1979 a study titled *Economic and Social Consequences of Nuclear Attacks on the United States* was published by the committee on banking, housing, and urban affairs of the U.S. Senate.[26] Going beyond the usual and often crude physical measures of destruction, such as human fatalities and casualties, number of cities destroyed, and damage to overall economic capacity, this study identifies and explores the interactive effects of nuclear attacks. As a result, it concludes as follows:

> A closer look at the "interactive" effects of various nuclear attacks leads to the conclusion that many studies of nuclear war in the open literature, which have been used to support policymaking, have underestimated the aggregate impact of a nuclear exchange on industrial states; particularly their ability to survive and recover their preattack position in a reasonable period of time. This understatement of the consequences results from concentration on simple quantitative indicators while ignoring interactive effects, such as the industrial example alluded to already. Similarly, casualty figures often include only victims of immediate blast or radiation effects, neglecting deaths traceable to the severe loss of medical facilities and personnel, which are heavily concentrated in the likely target areas. In a like manner, the ability of fallout or other shelters to save and preserve lives in urban areas has been overrated, as a result of an almost exclusive focus on initial blast or radiation hazards. This perspective understates the importance of side-effects (fire storms, exploding gas mains, lack of water supply, etc.) or longer-term effects (loss of adequate food supplies through production, processing or distribution failures, for example). In trying to establish minimum thresholds for national survival and recovery or criteria for nuclear attack acceptability, the adverse consequences of understating nuclear attack effects should be readily apparent.[27]

In May 1979, the Office of Technology Assessment of the U.S. Congress released its study *The Effects of Nuclear War.*[28] An assessment made in response to a request from the Senate committee on foreign relations to examine the effects of nuclear war on the populations and economies of the United States and the USSR, *The Effects of Nuclear War* explores the full range of effects that nuclear war would have on civilians. These effects include blast and radiation as well as indirect consequences from social, economic, and political disruption. Two of the study's major findings are that conditions would worsen over time after a nuclear war "ended" and that the effects of nuclear war that cannot be calculated in advance are at least as significant as those that can be calculated in advance. According to the introduction to the executive summary of the study:

> Throughout all the variations, possibilities, and uncertainties that this study describes, one theme is constant—a nuclear war would be a catastrophe. A militarily plausible nuclear attack, even "limited," could be expected to kill people and to inflict economic damage on a scale unprecedented in American experience; a large-scale nuclear exchange would be a calamity unprecedented in human history. The mind recoils from the effort to foresee the details of such a calamity, and from the careful explanation of the unavoidable uncertainties as to whether people would die from blast damage, from fallout radiation, or from starvation during the following winter. But the fact remains that nuclear war is possible, and the possibility of nuclear war has formed part of the foundation of international politics, and of U.S. policy, ever since nuclear weapons were used in 1945.[29]

Building upon some of the work found in *Economic and Social Consequences of Nuclear Attacks on the United States* and *The Effects of Nuclear War*, Kevin N. Lewis, in an article entitled "The Prompt and Delayed Effects of Nuclear War," further underscores the conclusion that "nuclear war remains an unmitigated mutual disaster, and that no conceivable civil-defense preparations could materially change the prospect."[30] Challenging the view that both of the superpowers need to be concerned about the integrity of their strategic retaliatory capabilities, Lewis points out that many of the most serious long-term effects are often ignored in discussions of "assured destruction." Alluding to the unpreventable consequences of economic devastation, Lewis demonstrates that all-out war remains a losing proposition for both sides. He concludes that "the cumulative effects of an all-out nuclear war would be so catastrophic that they render any notion of 'victory' meaningless."[31]

The idea that the concept of "victory" has no place in any form in a nuclear war is as old as the Atomic Age. In one of the first major theoretical treatments of the subject of nuclear war, Bernard Brodie wrote:

> The first and most vital step in any American security program for the age of atomic bombs is to take measures to guarantee to ourselves in case of attack the possibility of retaliation in kind. The writer in making this statement is not for the moment concerned about who will *win* the next war in which atomic bombs have been used. Thus far the chief purpose of our military establishment has been to win wars. From now on its chief purpose must be to avert them. It can have no other useful purpose.[32]

Even long before the Atomic Age, philosophers and military strategists probed the idea of victory with reasoned sensitivity. Machiavelli, for example, recognized the principle of an "economy of violence"[33] that distinguishes between creativity and destruction: "For it is the man who uses violence to spoil things, not the man who uses it to mend them, that is blameworthy."[34] With respect to war Machiavelli counseled that victory need not be in the best interests of the prince and that it might even produce an overall weakening of a state's position in international affairs.[35]

Unlike proponents of the "survival is possible" school, Machiavelli understood the difference between violence and power. More recently Hannah Arendt reflected on this distinction, elucidating a situation wherein the technical development of the implements of violence has outstripped any rational justifications for their use in armed conflict. Hence war is no longer the final arbiter in world politics, but rather an apocalyptic chess game that bears no resemblance to earlier games of power and domination. In such a game, if either wins both lose.[36]

Hannah Arendt's speculations on violence and power raise still another problem with the idea of victory in a nuclear war. This is the problem of arbitrariness or unpredictability intrinsic to all violence. Contrary to the anesthetized expectations of strategic thinkers who anticipate near perfect symmetry between human behavior and their own rarified strategic plans, violence harbors within itself an ineradicable element of the unexpected:

> nowhere does Fortuna, good or ill luck, play a more fateful role in human affairs than on the battlefield, and this intrusion of the utterly unexpected does not disappear when people call it a "random event" and find it scientifically suspect; nor can it be eliminated by simulations, scenarios, game theories, and the like. There is no certainty in these matters, not even an ultimate certainty of mutual destruction under certain calculated circumstances. The very fact that those engaged in the perfection of the means of destruction have finally reached a level of technical development where their aim, namely warfare, is on the point of disappearing altogether by virtue of the means at its disposal is like an ironical reminder of this all-pervading unpredictability, which we encounter the moment we approach the realm of violence.[37]

In this connection Arendt's concern for the uncertainties of violence stands in marked opposition to the ranks of all passionate systematizers who deny the essential irregularity of battlefield activity. In the fashion of modern historians who seek laws to explain and predict the vagaries of human conduct on a global scale, the strategists transform imperfect mosaics of military behavior into a structured logic of events. Entangled in false assumptions and ignored interactions, the proponents of forces that can "prevail" display a singular failure to understand the nonrational springs of action and feeling and an unreasonable degree of faith in game-theoretic systems of rational explanation. If only these strategic mythmakers could learn to appreciate how little humankind can control amid the disorderly multitude of factors involved in war. If only they could understand what presumptious hazards are associated with a strategy that seeks to impose order on what must inevitably be a heightened form of chaos.

Rejecting the myths of the strategists, students of world affairs must learn to disassociate any idea of victory from considerations of nuclear war. Even Clausewitz understood that war must be conducted with a view to postwar benefit and that the principle of "utmost force" must always be qualified by reference to "the political object." According to the master strategist, B.H. Liddell-Hart:

> The object in war is to attain a better peace—even if only from your own point of view. Hence it is essential to conduct war with constant regard to the peace you desire. This is the truth underlying Clausewitz's definition of war as "a continuation of policy by other means"—the prolongation of that policy through war into the subsequent peace must always be borne in mind. A state which expends its strength to the point of exhaustion bankrupts its own policy and future.[38]

Moreover, on victory, says Liddell-Hart:

> Victory in the true sense implies that the state of peace, and of one's people, is better after the war than before. Victory in this sense is only possible if a quick result can be gained or if a long effort can be economically proportioned to the national resources. The end must be adjusted to the means. Failing a fair prospect of such a victory, wise statesmanship will miss no opportunity for negotiating peace. Peace through stalemate, based on a coincident recognition by each side of the opponent's strength, is at least preferable to peace through common exhaustion—and has often provided a better foundation for lasting peace.[39]

Unlike the strategic mythmakers Liddell-Hart recognizes the futility of chasing victory when it is only a mirage. Challenging statesmen never to lose sight of the postwar prospect, he offers an intelligent counterweight to prescriptions for Armageddon. These views are seconded even by Henry Kissinger: "In the nuclear age, victory has lost its traditional significance. The *outbreak* of war is increasingly considered the worst catastrophe. Henceforth, the adequacy of any military establishment will be tested by its ability to preserve the peace."[40]

For this country's nuclear strategy to contribute effectively to the avoidance of nuclear war, it will have to emphasize that survival is not possible. Facing up to the gorgon's head of nuclear war is essential to avoidance of nuclear war. Rather than turning us into stone, an unflinching look at what is so often called unthinkable can reverse the encroachment of worldwide atomic catastrophe. Just as repressing the fear of death by individuals can occasion activities that impair the forces of self-preservation, so can this country impair its prospects for survival by insulating itself from reasonable fears of collective disintegration. Although it is true that the fear of death must be tempered in both individual and national drives lest it create paralysis, to deny the effect of such fear altogether is to make the threat of extinction more *imminent*.

While the strategic mythmakers pore tirelessly over their exegeses of nuclear doctrine, compiling an elaborate canon of elucidations, the planet moves steadily toward its final rendezvous with death. Lavishly subsidized by their government, which views costly plans for collective extermination as the best guarantee of peace, these tilters toward thanatos make a mockery of our genuine technological advances and of our capacity to endure as an intelligent species. No less misdirected because their speculations are pursued under official direction, their prescriptions for safety have already sunk into the vacuous pit of unreason.[41] To combat this cult of antilife, we must counter their facile calculations with an enlarged awareness of the cosmic deformations to which they may give rise. Armed with such an awareness, we can begin to respond to the cultivated falsifications of the strategic mythmakers with an informed counterblast of rejection and irreverence.

The urgency of such a response is reinforced by the peculiar character of the modern military megamachines. While earlier megamachines were kept limited by reliance upon manpower to exercise control, the new megamachines know no such limitations. Indeed, says Lewis Mumford, they "can command obedience and exert control through a vast battery of efficient machines, with fewer human intermediaries than ever before. To a degree hitherto impossible, the megamachine wears the magic cloak of invisibility: even its human servitors are emotionally protected by their remoteness from the human target they incinerate or obliterate."[42]

In this connection the prospect of nuclear war is also tied very closely to the *language* human beings have adopted for strategic studies. Such euphemisms as "crisis relocation," "limited nuclear war," "collateral damage," "countervalue" and "counterforce" strategies, and "enhanced radiation warfare"[43] are insidious to the cause of peace because they tend to make the currency of nuclear war-fighting valid coin. Just as the barbarisms of the Nazis were made possible through such linguistic disguises as "final solution," "resettlement," "special treatment," and "selections," so do the euphemisms of the nuclear age make nuclear war more likely. To counter the current euphemisms that may etherize an unwitting humanity into accepting nuclear war, humankind must come to understand how much it is already lost in its own gibberish. In doing this, the species may eradicate a major obstacle to survival.

Notes

1. Gray and Payne, "Victory Is Possible," *Foreign Policy*, no. 39, Summer 1980, p. 14. Curiously Gray and Payne also base their argument on the just-war doctrine of the Catholic Church. This reliance upon the doctrine of the just war is misconceived for two basic reasons. First, this doctrine, based upon the teachings of St. Augustine and St. Thomas Aquinas and refined by such scholars as de Vitoria, Suarez, Grotius, Pufendorf, Wolff and Vattel, is logically irrelevant to the Gray–Payne argument and has been discredited and disregarded since the end of the eighteenth century. According to long-standing international law, every use of force is always judged twice: with reference to both the reasons for fighting and to the means adopted. It follows that even if an argument can be made for going to war according to the principles of *jus ad bellum* (justice of war), the resort to nuclear weapons would be contrary to the principles of *jus in bello*. This conclusion is supported by such authoritative sources of international law (according to article 38 of the Statute of the International Court of Justice) as the Hague and Geneva conventions, the principles of international law recognized by the charter of the Nuremberg Tribunal and the judgment of the tribunal, the corpus of international custom from which these conventions and principles derive, the general principles of law recognized by civilized nations, and the Shimoda decision by the Tokyo district court of Japan in 1955, which held that the nuclear attacks on Hiroshima and Nagasaki were in violation of international law because: (1) the indiscriminate bombing of undefended cities is forbiddden by international law, (2) the bombing of the two Japanese cities was not a result of "military necessity," (3) the cities were not "military targets" and (4) the bombs occasioned even more suffering than those weapons already outlawed for producing "unnecessary and cruel forms of suffering." Second, there is nothing in the extant law of the UN Charter or in the elucidation of that law in the 1974 UN General Assembly definition of aggression to support their position on nuclear war. For a full consideration of the relevance of international law to the use of nuclear weapons, see Richard A. Falk, Lee Meyrowitz, and Jack Sanderson, *Nuclear Weapons and International Law*, World Order Studies Program, Occasional Paper 10, Center of International Studies, Princeton University, 1981; and Richard A. Falk and Robert Jay Lifton, *Indefensible Weapons* (New York: Basic Books, 1983).

2. Ibid., p. 25.

3. On this point see Bernard T. Feld and Kosta Tsipis, "Land-Based Intercontinental Ballistic Missiles," *Scientific American* 241, no. 5 (November 1979): 51–61; and Kosta Tsipis, "The Accuracy of Strategic Missiles," *Scientific American* 233, no. 1. (July 1975): 14–23.

4. The following are some current and projected improvements in C^3I, based upon information in "Preparing for Nuclear War: President Reagan's Program," Center for Defense Information, *The Defense Monitor* 10, no. 8 (1982): 14:

E-4B advanced airborne national command post (AABNCP)—a modified 747 aircraft enabling the president to command U.S. nuclear forces from the air during a nuclear crisis

Strategic Air Command digital network (SACDIN)—survivable communications between SAC headquarters and missiles or bombers

MILSTAR extremely high frequency (EHF) communications satellite

Ground-based electrooptical deep space surveillance system (GEODSS)—satellite monitoring

Two additional PAVE PAWS sites—early warning of SLBM (Submarine Launched Ballistic Missile) launches

Air force satellite communications (AFSATCOM)—Allows the President and military commanders to communicate with and send orders to U.S. nuclear forces

Extremely low frequency (ELF) system—Communications with submarines)

Satellite survivability enhancement

5. See *Hearings*, November 9, 1981, on "Strategic Weapons Proposals," *Hearings* before the Committee on Foreign Relations, United States Senate, 97th Congress, 1st Session, on The Foreign Policy and Arms Control Implications of President Reagan's Strategic Weapons Proposals, U.S. Government Printing Office, Washington, D.C. 1981. p. 110. Warnke's "discomfort" may not be as hard to document as he thinks. For example, on January 13, 1981, Deputy Secretary of Defense Frank Carlucci made the following remark: "I think we need to have a counterforce capability. Over and above that, I think that we need to have a warfighting capability." And on November 3, 1981, Secretary of Defense Weinberger stated: "We set out to . . . achieve improved capabilities to enhance deterrence and U.S. capabilities to prevail should deterrence fail." See Center for Defense

Information, "Preparing for Nuclear War: President Reagan's Program," *The Defense Monitor* 10, no. 8 (1982).

6. Ibid., p. 135. In a later portion of his testimony, Admiral Carroll documents his concerns by citing various remarks of Secretary of Defense Weinberger and of Undersecretary of Defense (Research and Engineering) Richard DeLauer. According to Carroll, DeLauer recently endorsed the Trident II missile because it would give the U.S. "preemptive capability" to attack Soviet forces such as missile silos, ibid., p. 140.

7. See "An Open Letter to President Carter and Chairman Brezhnev," Physicians for Social Responsibility, *PSR Newsletter* 1, no. 2 (April 1980):1. This letter is a summary for informed laypersons of more technical studies undertaken by Physicians for Social Responsibility (PSR). These studies are the product of a series of symposia sponsored by PSR and affiliated groups on the subject of "The Medical Consequences of Nuclear Weapons and Nuclear War." Similarly, scholarly studies of the effects of nuclear war have been undertaken by International Physicians for the Prevention of Nuclear War, a group of prominent physicians modeled after the Pugwash Movement. The June-July 1981 issue of *The Bulletin of the Atomic Scientists* (37, no. 6) is dedicated entirely to the writings of the international community of physicians on nuclear war, the ultimate medical emergency.

8. Herbert L. Abrams, "Infection and Communicable Diseases," in *The Final Epidemic: Physicians and Scientists on Nuclear War,* edited by Ruth Adams and Susan Cullen (Chicago: Educational Foundation for Nuclear Science, 1981), p. 201.

9. Robert Jay Lifton and Eric Olson, *Living and Dying* (New York: Praeger, 1974), p. 129.

10. See *The Myth of the Machine,* p. 302.

11. This testimony, offered on June 19, 1980, is cited in "The Race to Nuclear War," *The Defense Monitor*, 11 no. 6 (1980): 1–8.

12. For more information concerning the effects of a nuclear attack on Washington, see *PSR Newsletter*, Physicians for Social Responsibility, 3, no. 3., (Cambridge, Mass.: Fall 1982).

13. See Special Study Section of the Physicians for Social Responsiblity, "The Medical Consequences of Thermonuclear War," *The New England Journal of Medicine* 266 (1962):1126–55.

14. See, for example, Jack Geiger, "Addressing Apocalypse Now, The Effects of Nuclear Warfare as a Public Health Concern," *American Journal of Public Health* 70 (1980) 958–81. Geiger's comments emphasize the unpredictable longer range effects of a nuclear war.

15. In this connection, no attention was paid to the consequences of the destruction of nuclear energy plants in war. For an authoritative and up-to-date assessment of such consequences, see Bennett Ramberg, *Destruction*

of Nuclear Energy Facilities in War: The Problem and the Implications (Lexington, Mass.: Lexington Books, D.C. Heath, 1980).

16. For a current example of this effort, see Bernard Lown, Eric Chivian, James Muller, and Herbert Abrams, "Sounding Board: The Nuclear Arms Race and the Physician," *The New England Journal of Medicine* 304 (March 19, 1981): 726–29.

17. Course material will include the physics and delivery of weapons systems; the biological and ecological effects of radiation, blast, and intense heat; and postattack medical and psychosocial needs and likely remaining medical resources. Also considered will be the psychosocial implications of living under the continual threat of nuclear annihilation, and the international psychology supporting the nuclear arms race. Lecturers have been drawn from the faculties of Harvard University and the Massachusetts Institute of Technology.

Weekly sessions are scheduled as follows: (1) Delivery Systems and Technology, Thomas Halstead of the anti–nuclear weapons group of PSR; (2) Physics of Weaponry and Effect on Ecology, Kosta Tsipis, research associate in physics at MIT; (3) Background; History of War and Nuclear Weapons, Everett Mendelsohn, professor of the history of science at Harvard University; (4) Effect of One-Megaton Bomb/of All-Out War, by Leaf; (5) Nature and Problems of Fallout, Henry Kendall, professor of physics at MIT and president of the Union of Concerned Scientists; (6) Protective Measures—Active, Passive, Civil, Eric Chivian, staff psychiatrist at MIT; (7) Biological Effects, Including Radiation Sickness, Herbert Abrams, Cook professor of radiology at Harvard Medical School (HMS).

Also (8) Blast Damage and Burns, John Constable, HMS Associate Clinical Professor of Surgery; (9) Medical Problems of Survivors, Dr. Abrams; (10) "Long-Term Biological Effects," Samuel Latt, professor of pediatrics at HMS and a geneticist; (11) Food and Malnutrition in a Post-Attack World, instructor to be announced; (12) and (13) Psychological/Social Aspects of Nuclear Warfare, John Mack, HMS professor of psychiatry at the Cambridge Hospital, and James E. Muller, assistant professor of medicine at Brigham and Women's Hospital; (14) Economic Impact of Arms Race, John Kenneth Galbraith, Warburg professor of economics emeritus at Harvard; and (15) The Role of Physicians in Education on the Health Issues of Nuclear War, a faculty panel.

18. See "Special Report: Medical Problems of Survivors of Nuclear War," *The New England Journal of Medicine* 305 (November 12, 1981): 1226–32. The authors are Herbert L. Abrams and William E. Von Kaenel, both of the Harvard Medical School. This paper represents a shortened version of a chapter by Abrams in *The Final Epidemic: Physicians and Scientists on Nuclear War*, edited by Ruth Adams and Susan Cullen (Chicago: The Educational Foundaton for Nuclear Science, 1981), pp.

192–218. This piece is entitled, "Infection and Communicable Diseases," and is part of a volume that offers particularly extensive and authoritative information on the health consequences of a nuclear war.

19. For the authoritative assessment of the effects of the Hiroshima bomb, see *Hiroshima and Nagasaki: The Physical, Medical and Social Effects of the Atomic Bombings* (New York: Basic Books, 1981), a report by the Committee for the Compilation of Materials on Damage Caused by the Atomic Bombings in Hiroshima and Nagasaki.

20. See p. 1226.

21. See p. 1228; the internal citation refers to Cresson H. Kearny, *Nuclear War Survival Skills*, ORNL-5037, Oak Ridge National Laboratory, Oak Ridge, Tenn., 1979, pp. 94–95; and R.U. Ayres, *Environmental Effects of Nuclear Weapons*, The Hudson Institute, Croton on Hudson, N.Y., 1965, Office of Civil Defense Report no. HI-518RR.

22. See p. 1229.

23. See Handler's letter of transmittal, which is contained at the beginning of the report.

24. Ibid.

25. This point has aroused considerable controversy, causing the Federation of American Scientists to charge NAS with having reached a "false conclusion."

26. Study prepared for the joint committee on defense production.

27. See the Executive Summary, pp. 1–2.

28. See no.OTA-NS-89, Washington, D.C.

29. Ibid., p.3.

30. See *Scientific American* 241, no. 1 (July 1979): p. 35.

31. Ibid., p. 47.

32. See Bernard Brodie, ed., *The Absolute Weapon* (New York: Harcourt, Brace, 1946), p. 76.

33. See the discussion of this principle in Sheldon S. Wolin, *Politics and Vision: Continuity and Innovation in Western Political Thought* (Boston: Little, Brown, 1960), pp. 195–238.

34. See *Discourses*, I, cited by Wolin, *Politics and Vision,* p. 221.

35. See *Discourses,* II, cited by Wolin, *Politics and Vision,* p. 222.

36. See Hannah Arendt, *On Violence* (New York: Harcourt, Brace, and World, 1970), p.3.

37. Ibid., pp. 4–5.

38. See B.H. Liddell-Hart, *Strategy,* 2nd rev. ed. (New York: The New American Library, 1974), p. 353.

39. Ibid., p. 357.

40. See Henry Kissinger, *The Necessity for Choice: Prospects of American Foreign Policy* (Garden City: N.Y., Doubleday, Anchor, 1962), p. 12.

41. As an example of this imbecility, the Department of Defense has announced a plan to obtain the cooperation of civilian hospitals in the event of a nuclear war. According to this plan (Civilian Military Contingency Hospitalization System, or CMCHS), each of these hospitals will be asked to commit at least fifty beds to the expected victims. Fortunately the medical community has reacted to this plan with appropriate incredulity and derision. Calling the plan "profoundly unrealistic," PSR, on October 15, 1981, called upon hospital administrators and medical staff to reject it.

42. Mumford, *The Myth of the Machine* (New York: Harcourt, Brace, Jovanovich, 1970), p. 267.

43. To summarize these concepts:

> *Limited nuclear war* refers to a measured and strictly controlled strategic exchange confined to military and industrial targets. The consequences of such a war, if it were a real possibility, could involve tens of millions of fatalities.
>
> *Collateral damage* refers to the damage done to human and nonhuman resources as a consequence of strategic strikes directed at enemy forces or military facilities. This "unintended" damage could involve tens of millions of fatalities.
>
> *Countervalue strategies* refer to targeting of an opponent's cities or industries—the targeting of millions of innocent civilians.
>
> *Counterforce strategies* refer to targeting of an adversary's strategic military facilities. Such strategies are dangerous not only because of the "collateral damage" that they might produce but also because they heighten the likelihood of first-strike attacks.
>
> *Enhanced radiation warfare* refers to the use of thermonuclear weapons (commonly called neutron bombs) that kill primarily through the distribution of radioactive neutrons while leaving buildings and other structures intact.

5 Arms Control

The fourth principal assumption of current American nuclear strategy is that a major arms buildup can be undertaken without compromising the prospects for vertical and horizontal arms control. Yet it is clear that the countervailing nuclear strategy requires supporting strategic weapons systems that must preclude any Soviet–American START accord. And since such an accord is essential to the success of the nonproliferation regime, this strategy also contributes to the spread of nuclear weapons to other countries.

According to the terms of the Treaty on the Nonproliferation of Nuclear Weapons, the superpowers are obligated to move expeditiously toward meaningful arms control and disarmament. In the words of Article 6 of the treaty:

> Each of the Parties to the Treaty undertakes to pursue negotiations in good faith on effective measures relating to cessation of the nuclear arms race at an early date and to nuclear disarmament, and on a treaty on general and complete disarmament under strict and effective international control.

In the absence of American compliance with Article 6, it is difficult to imagine that nonnuclear weapon states will continue their restricted condition indefinitely. This point is supported by the results of the latest nonproliferation treaty review conference, which ended in September 1980 after developing countries accused the superpowers of failing to reduce their strategic arsenals.[1] Should the United States proceed with its countervailing nuclear strategy, the prospects for negotiated arms limitation with the USSR would become nil. The resultant spread of nuclear weapon states not only would create new opportunities for nuclear conflict but also would heighten the probability of a Soviet–American nuclear war. This is the case because of the increased likelihood of catalytic war (war provoked by a new nuclear power), war between new nuclear powers with alliance or interest ties to the superpowers, and nuclear terrorism.

On July 16, 1981, President Reagan formally announced his administration's policy on limiting the spread of nuclear weapons. Describing nonproliferation as "a fundamental national security and foreign policy objective," the president emphasized three major guidelines:

> Efforts will be made "to improve regional and global stability" in order to "reduce motivations" that drive countries to develop nuclear weapons.

> Efforts will be made to expand "international cooperation" as an "essential part" of nonproliferation activities.
>
> Efforts will be made to revive the American role as a "reliable nuclear supplier" of nuclear technology for "peaceful nuclear cooperation under adequate safeguards."[2]

While this statement was designed to correct what the president called the "false impression" that the Reagan administration is not strongly committed to nonproliferation objectives, it does nothing to indicate American support for Article 6 of the treaty. Indeed the president's stated commitment to "Strive to reduce the motivation for acquiring nuclear explosives by working to improve regional and global stability and to promote understanding of the legitimate security concerns of other states" is a thinly veiled reaffirmation of American reliance on theater nuclear forces. Such reliance is not only needlessly provocative to the Soviet Union, it is fundamentally inconsistent with the requirements of superpower arms control.

Without a serious and explicit commitment to the imperatives of article 6, the Reagan administration's policy on nonproliferation is destined to fail. To create such a commitment, a basic transformation must take place in the flawed notion that arms control can wait until we achieve a "position of strength." It is to be hoped that this transformation was set into motion with the commencement of START (Strategic Arms Reduction Talks) on June 29, 1982.

The United States could begin to take additional steps toward arms control and nonproliferation by rejecting once and for all, the dangerously misconceived notion of "linkage." Contrary to the administration's intermittent claims that American willingness to progress in arms talks is essentially a concession contingent upon Soviet compliance with this country's expectations, such willingness is also essential to *our* survival. An incontestable mutuality of interest in arms control exists. There is no reason to believe that the United States is in any better position than the USSR to avoid nuclear war via the time-dishonored principles of *realpolitik*. This point was clearly understood by Paul C. Warnke:

> A SALT II Treaty or any other arms control agreement between the Soviet Union and the United States certainly should not be a reward for Soviet good behavior. We should enter into any arms control agreement if—and only if—it advances U.S. security interests when viewed on its own merits.[3]

And it was well understood by the writers of a recent editorial in *The New York Times*, who said that insisting upon a political agreement first is "a prescription, or a pretext, for an uncontrolled and disastrous arms race."[4]

The underlying rationale of current American nuclear strategy can be summed up as follows: In a world system that lacks government, right is coincident with power. Therefore each state must do what it can to strengthen its relative power position. Indeed in a world situation of "all against all," each state is obligated to pursue national goals on a competitive basis and to strive continually for maximum strength and influence.

The problem with this "realist" kind of thinking (an international relations legacy from Thucydides to Morgenthau and beyond) is that it is strikingly unrealistic. It generates a spiral of fear and mistrust that inhibits general cooperation, then freezes developing hostilities into fixed and intransigent camps, and explodes ultimately into general warfare. This fear and mistrust feeds back to world leaders and reinforces the commitment to a "get what you can" philosophy of international conduct. All in all, realism is exceptionally naive. I say naive because, as George F. Kennan said at Dartmouth College upon receiving the Grenville Clark prize "there is a naivete of cynicism and suspicion just as there is a naivete of innocence."[5]

The militaristic nations in world politics coexist in the manner of a group of herders who share a common pasture and who feel it advantageous to increase the size of their respective herds. Although these herders have calculated that it is in their own best interests continuously to enlarge their herds, they have calculated incorrectly. They have done so because they have failed to consider the *cumulative effect* of their calculations: an overgrazed commons and economic ruin.

In the fashion of the herdsmen in this analogy, the Reagan administration continues to act as if the security of the United States is coincident with continued increases and improvements in strategic military forces. Like the herdsmen the failure of the administration to understand the cumulative effects of its reasoning leads this country farther and farther away from the intended condition (in this case, of real security). Blithely unaware that its strategy of "realism" is strikingly unrealistic, the administration's search for an improved strategic power position vis-à-vis the Soviet Union will inevitably generate Soviet countermoves that nullify any force improvements and inhibit any remaining opportunities for essential cooperation.

This conclusion is supported by patterns of Soviet military spending. As has been pointed out by Richard Barnet:

> defense spending is an index of intentions. That the Soviets are willing year after year to devote to the military establishment a considerably higher fraction of their considerably smaller national wealth suggests that they are determined to stay in the arms race and that they will never again willingly revert to a position of obvious military inferiority.[6]

Since the USSR will never stand still for the United States and allow it to achieve its current strategic objectives, the Reagan administration will *never* be prepared for genuine arms reductions. By arming for arms control, the United States will inevitably make arms control impossible. This argument is underscored by the action-reaction dynamics of the nuclear arms race to date[7]:

Action ⇄ Reaction
in the nuclear competition

The dynamics of the nuclear arms race ensure that development of a new weapons system by one power will in a relatively brief period be followed by a comparable achievement by the other. Both powers have had firsts. Neither has stayed ahead for long. The United States generally has a technological lead of several years, but the futility of the race for short-term advantage is demonstrated by a chronology of developments to date.

U.S. 1945 atomic bomb 1949 USSR

The nuclear age began with the explosion of a U.S. A-bomb of 12.5 kilotons (equivalent to 12,500 tons of TNT) over Hiroshima, Japan. The single bomb, which destroyed the city, introduced to the world a concentrated explosive force of unprecedented power. Within four years the USSR conducted its first atomic test.

U.S. 1948 intercontinental bomber 1955 USSR

By 1948 the United States had begun to replace the propeller planes of World War II with long-range jets. The first planes developed for strategic bombing required refueling to reach another continent. In 1955 the United States began deployment of the all-jet intercontinental bomber, and the USSR soon followed suit.

U.S. 1954 hydrogen bomb 1955 USSR

The H-bomb multiplied the explosive force of the A-bomb 1,000 times. The first U.S. thermonuclear bomb had a yield equivalent to 15 million tons of TNT; a year later the USSR tested a bomb in the million-ton range.

USSR 1957 intercontinental ballistic missile (ICBM) 1958 U.S.

Following intensive development by both nuclear powers, a land-based missile to carry nuclear warheads intercontinental distances was successfully flight tested by the USSR in 1957, and by the United States one year later. By 1962 both nations had ICBMs with a range of 6,000 miles, each missile able to carry a payload equivalent to 5–10 million tons of TNT.

USSR 1957	man-made satellite in orbit	1958 U.S.

Sputnik I by the USSR initiated a space race that quickly took on military functions; the first U.S. satellite was launched into orbit the following year. Well over half the superpowers' satellites have been military: for surveillance, targeting, communications, and so on.

U.S. 1960	submarine-launched ballistic missile (SLBM)	1968 USSR

A nuclear-powered submarine that could fire long-range missiles from a submerged position was the third means of strategic delivery. The United States produced the nuclear-powered Polaris, with missiles with a range of 1,200 nautical miles. Eight years later the USSR had comparable nuclear subs.

U.S. 1966	multiple warhead (MRV)	1968 USSR

Multiheaded missiles increased the number of targets a missile could hit. U.S. MRVed missiles carried three warheads, each with 16 times the explosive force of the Hiroshima bomb. The USSR had them two years later.

USSR 1968	antiballistic missile (ABM)	1972 U.S.

The USSR deployed 64 defensive missiles around Moscow. The United States began construction of the Safeguard system in 1969 and had one site completed when a treaty restricting ABMs was signed in 1972. Generally judged militarily ineffective, ABMs were restricted to one site in each country in 1974. Subsequently the U.S. site was closed.

U.S. 1970	multiple independently targeted warhead (MIRV)	1975 USSR

Further development of multiple warheads enabled one missile to hit three to ten individually selected targets as far apart as 100 miles. The USSR began to flight test MIRVs three years after the United States put them in service and in 1975 began deployment.

U.S. 1982	long-range cruise missile	198? USSR

Adaptable to launching from air, sea, and land, a new generation of missiles with a range up to 1,500 miles is in production. The cruise missile is small, relatively inexpensive, highly accurate, with the unique advantage of very low trajectory. Following the contours of the earth and flying under radar, it will be able to destroy its target without warning. The United States is reportedly seven to ten years in the lead in this technology.

U.S. 1983 neutron bomb 198? USSR

This nuclear weapon releases its explosive energy more in the form of an invisible, penetrating bombardment of radiation rather than in heat and blast. The decision to produce and stockpile the enhanced radiation warhead in the United States was announced in August 1981. The USSR promptly announced that it has the capability but had deferred a production decision.

U.S. 199? antisatellite weapons 199? USSR

Because satellites play vital military roles, they have also inspired a search for weapons to destroy them. The USSR began testing intercepter satellites in 1968. Both superpowers are attempting to perfect lasers to destroy enemy satellites and nuclear missiles in event of war.

According to testimony of Admiral Eugene Carroll, Jr., before the U.S. Senate committee on foreign relations:

> Fundamental to the Reagan nuclear program is the assumption that the path to real arms control and stability lies through a big buildup of U.S. nuclear forces in order to conduct negotiations from a position of strength. Obviously, strong U.S. forces must be maintained to permit successful negotiations. But there is no historical evidence to suggest that a single-minded "muscle-flexing" will result in Soviet docility and force them to accede to our desires and preferences. The Soviets will certainly not allow us to achieve a "break-out" in nuclear forces. They have sacrificed a great deal to achieve rough equivalence in strategic nuclear forces and will continue to do so. The most likely Soviet response to our $180 billion program is one of their own, featuring new generations of nuclear weapons systems to match ours. The Soviet leadership will undoubtedly perceive our stepped-up efforts as a challenge to their security which must be met, and the escalatory spiral of the arms race will continue.[8]

Before current American nuclear strategy can be rendered compatible with the imperatives of superpower arms control and nonproliferation, the Reagan administration must abandon its planned deployment of strategic weapons with hard-target kill capabilities. As has already been noted, the additive effects of Trident II and MX could put a large portion of Soviet fixed ICBMs at risk. According to the U.S. Arms Control and Disarmament Agency, "This could have significant destabilizing effects, and thus a potential negative arms control impact."[9]

Moreover, the administration must carefully avoid taking any measures that could lead to renunciation of the ABM treaty. The danger is real that the United States may seek to protect its MX forces by the deployment of a ballistic missile defense system. Should such deployment take place, the resultant ABM Treaty termination would be widely interpreted as an American violation of Article 6 of the NPT. It follows that such deployment would be injurious to a sound American nonproliferation policy. Consider the following assessment of the ABM treaty and national security by the Committee for National Security:

> Arms control is a critical component of national security policy that must not be abandoned. The most significant arms control agreement to date—the 1972 Treaty on the Limitation of Anti-Ballistic Missile Systems—is in danger and needs to be preserved.
>
> *The ABM Treaty is of vital importance to our national security*. The 1972 Treaty accomplishes much that we want in the area of arms control. Although the bilateral treaty is of unlimited duration, the Soviets and the U.S. review it at five-year intervals. . . . The Treaty's abrogation would represent a grave blow to arms control and, therefore, to our security.
>
>> The ABM Treaty is the most important strategic arms control agreement we have. If we and the Soviets amend or abrogate the ABM Treaty, and deploy a defensive system, the result would be an acceleration of the strategic arms race which neither side can win;
>>
>> Recent technological developments may tempt some in Congress and the Administration to support abrogation of the Treaty in order to deploy new types of ABMs such as Low Altitude Defense Systems (LoADs), a "layered defense," or space-based lasers. Some Pentagon officials argue that the only way to protect a land-based missile will be with an ABM system such as LoADs. The Reagan Administration has cancelled the MX racetrack, avoided the bureaucratic battles associated with a submarine-based MX, and is considering deploying an ABM system to allay fears that the MX would not be able to survive the threat of thousands of Soviet warheads;
>>
>> Abrogating the Treaty could lead to a city defense system both in the U.S. and the USSR. The Soviets already have their small ABM system located around Moscow. Heavy pressures would develop for the U.S. to defend its cities for the "modest" additional cost and to match the Soviet defense. Yet a city defense would be a mirage, since it demands 100 percent effectiveness; no one claims such effectiveness for any ABM system;
>>
>> Abrogation of the Treaty and subsequent deployment of an ABM system would provide an enormous incentive to strike first. Were we to strike first, it could be argued, we would have a full force with which to attack, saturate their ABM system and destroy the other country. It could be argued to the President that their retaliatory strike would then not be big enough to penetrate our ABMs. The Soviets would

have the same first-strike incentive. The ABM Treaty itself substantially removes the incentive for either side to strike first. With the Treaty, neither side can take away the other's ability to retaliate massively;

Abrogating the ABM Treaty would have an unfortunate impact on the proliferation of nuclear weapons. ABM deployments would be viewed as further escalations in the arms race and, therefore, would undermine the Nonproliferation Treaty, which states in Article VI that each party (including the U.S. and USSR) "undertakes to pursue negotiations in good faith on effective measures relating to the cessation of the nuclear arms race at an early date..." Scrapping the principal accomplishment of SALT I would certainly put into question our intention to live up to Article VI of the NPT;

It is not necessary to abrogate the Treaty in order to protect the fixed land-based missiles. The Committee for National Security contends that the supposed Soviet capacity to attack the Minuteman force is not a capability with any strategic or diplomatic value. Scenarios in which they take advantage of alleged "Minuteman vulnerability" are simply not credible. The best way to deal with such scenarios is through significant reductions in "first-strike" missiles. Rather than considering abrogating the ABM Treaty, the United States should build on it in negotiating a new offensive strategic arms limitation agreement.[10]

We see, therefore, that an American ABM deployment would degrade the stability of deterrence between the superpowers. This is the case because it would generate a parallel Soviet deployment of ballistic missile defense systems, which would in turn generate a mutual search for new offensive missile capabilities. Taken together, such developments would heighten each side's fear of a first strike by the other, and would undermine any remaining prospects for the negotiation of a strategic arms control agreement.

The failure of the START process would have additional corrosive effects on superpower arms control efforts. One such effect would be the end of negotiations on long-range theater nuclear forces in Europe. The United States is now embarked on negotiations with the USSR on long-range theater nuclear forces as part of the arrangement under which NATO states have agreed to accept European-based American missiles targeted on the Soviet Union. The failure of START would make it impossible to succeed with such negotiations. This is the case because it would be purposeless to attempt to negotiate limits on Soviet medium and intermediate-range missiles if the Soviets are free to deploy as many ICBMs as they wish and target them against Western Europe.[11]

A second arms control casualty of the failure of START would be the end of negotiations to bar testing and deployment of antisatellite (ASAT) weapons systems. Without a START agreement, ASAT competition would undoubtedly continue, thereby heightening tensions and fear of a first strike. The resultant space weapons race would produce increased temptations to each side to preempt since destruction of certain satellite capabilities would leave the victim nation blind.

Regrettably the START negotiations commenced in Geneva shortly after the Reagan administration announced that it had already abandoned the search for an antisatellite agreement. In spite of the president's expressed concern at Eureka College on May 9, 1982 for the "growing instability of the nuclear balance," it is apparent that he disassociates this concern from the proliferation of antisatellite weapons. Thus in early June 1982, acting on orders from the president, Secretary of Defense Weinberger directed the U.S. Air Force to prepare to deploy antisatellite weapons within five years. Taken together with the formal strategy of protracted nuclear war with the USSR, this directive reveals the continuing lack of commitment to principles of arms control.

The United States is already accelerating development of weapons designed to destroy enemy satellites. Among the several components of such development efforts, the most significant near term program appears to be the miniature homing intercept vehicle, a small device that would home in on the infrared radiation of a target satellite. The U.S. ASAT program will also pursue methods for attacking satellites in high and geosynchronous orbits of about 22,300 miles, where many major military satellites are stationed.

Although ASAT weapons are attractive to the military because destruction of enemy satellites would eliminate important military capabilities of an adversary, they also add to the complexity and cost of the arms race and further complicate arms control measures. Thus they heighten the probability of the war they are intended to help fight. Moreover it is clear that ASAT weapons would not move armed conflicts into outer space, thereby preventing mass destruction on earth. Although the proliferation of such weapons may mean that the next war will *begin* in space, it will surely not end on that high frontier.[12]

Current American nuclear strategy cannot be reconciled with the requirements of strategic arms control and nonproliferation. To satisfy these requirements, thereby enhancing the prospects of nuclear war avoidance, the United States must take immediate steps to forswear nuclear weapons programs and associated policies that generate fear and insecurity in the USSR and elsewhere. Concurrent with these steps, the government should begin restoring the entire arms control agenda to a position of primacy in superpower strategic relations.[13] It is essential to keep in mind that efforts to control nuclear armaments have been underway since 1946 (when the United States proposed placing all such weapons under international authority) and that these efforts have produced a vital "regime" of treaties to prevent nuclear war:

Treaties to Control Nuclear Weapons[14]

To prevent the spread of nuclear weapons—

Antarctic Treaty — December 1, 1959 — 22 states
Bans any military uses of Antarctica and specifically prohibits nuclear tests and waste.

Outer Space Treaty — January 27, 1967 — 76 states
Bans nuclear weapons in earth orbit and their stationing in outer space.

Latin American Nuclear-Free Zone Treaty — February 14, 1967 — 22 states
Bans testing, possession, deployment, of nuclear weapons and requires safeguards on facilities. All Latin American states except Argentina, Brazil, Chile, Cuba, are parties to the treaty.

Non-Proliferation Treaty — July 1, 1968 — 115 states
Bans transfer of weapons or weapons technology to non-nuclear-weapons states. Requires safeguards on their facilities. Commits nuclear-weapon states to negotiations to halt the arms race.

Seabed Treaty — February 11, 1971 — 66 states
Bans nuclear weapons on the seabed beyond a 12-mile coastal limit.

To reduce the risk of nuclear war between the U.S. and USSR—

Hot Line Agreement and Modernization — June 20, 1963 — US-USSR Agreement
Establishes direct radio and wire-telegraph links between Moscow and Washington to ensure communication between heads of government in times of crisis. A second agreement in 1971 provided for satellite communication circuits to improve reliability.

Accidents Measures Agreement — September 30, 1971 — US-USSR
Pledges U.S. and USSR to improve safeguards against accidental or unauthorized use of nuclear weapons.

Prevention of Nuclear War Agreement — June 22, 1973 — US-USSR
Requires consultation between the two countries if there is a danger of nuclear war.

To limit nuclear testing—

Partial Test Ban Treaty — August 5, 1963 — 108 states[a]
Bans nuclear weapons tests in the atmosphere, outer space, or underwater. Bans underground explosions which cause release of radioactive debris beyond the state's borders.

Threshhold Test Ban Treaty — July 3, 1974 — US-USSR[b]
Bans underground tests having a yield above 150 kilotons (150,000 tons of TNT).

Peaceful Nuclear Explosions Treaty — May 28, 1976 — US-USSR[b]
Bans "group explosions" with aggregate yield over 1,500 kilotons and requires on-site observers of group explosions with yield over 150 kilotons.

To limit nuclear weapons—

ABM Treaty (SALT I) and Protocol May 26, 1972 US-USSR
Limits anti-ballistic missile systems to two deployment areas on each side. Subsequently, in Protocol of 1974, each side was restricted to one deployment area.

Salt I Interim Agreement May 26, 1972 US-USSR
Freezes the number of strategic ballistic missile launchers, and permits an increase in SLBM launchers up to an agreed level only with equivalent dismantling of older ICBM or SLBM launchers.

SALT II June 18, 1979 US-USSR[b]
Limits numbers of strategic nuclear delivery vehicles, launchers of MIRV'd missiles, bombers with long-range cruise missiles, warheads on existing ICBM's, etc. Bans testing or deploying new ICBM's.

[a]number of accessions and ratifications. [b]not yet ratified

If this regime of international legal agreements is to endure and become progressively more effective, the adversary relationship between the United States and the Soviet Union must not be modeled after the conflict between the Archangels Michael and Lucifer. Rather than continue to base American foreign policy on a Manichean view of good versus evil, the U.S. government must learn to build upon the realization that the adversaries share a joint and irreversible commitment to the avoidance of nuclear war. A warning offered by George F. Kennan warrants special attention. Although recognizing that much in the Soviet system is unpalatable, Kennan observes that the view of the USSR presented to the American public by government and press is dangerously subjective and oversimplified, that it routinely exaggerates Soviet military capabilities and the nefariousness of Soviet intentions. He refers to the U.S. refusal to acknowledge common concerns, problems, and goals, and concludes that these attitudes are not worthy of a great and powerful state.[15]

The reasonableness of Kennan's views is underscored by the historical role of the United States in the technological arms race. According to Herbert York, whose professional life has been involved with the arms race at very high levels:

> Our [U.S.] unilateral decisions have set the rate and scale for most of the individual steps in the strategic arms race. In many cases we started development before they did and we easily established a large and long-lasting lead in terms of deployed numbers and types. Examples include the A-bomb itself, intercontinental bombers, submarine-launched ballistic missiles, and MIRV. In other instances, the first development steps were taken by the two sides at about the same time, but immediately afterward our program ran well ahead of theirs both in the development of further types and applications and in the deployment of large numbers. Such cases include the mighty H-bomb, and, very probably, military space applica-

> tions. In some cases, to be sure, they started developing work ahead of us and arrived first at the stage where they were able to commence deployment. But we usually reacted so strongly that our deployments and capabilities soon ran far ahead of theirs and we, in effect, even here, determined the final size of the operation.[16]

And where has it gotten us? In what must surely be the single greatest irony in the history of our species, our participation in the nuclear arms race has made us progressively more insecure. Today after the expenditure of trillions of dollars on armaments and the creation of arsenals housing over 9,000 strategic nuclear weapons, each thousands of times more powerful than the Hiroshima/Nagasaki bombs, we are entirely indefensible.

Moreover, American military spending has degraded our national security by its steady deterioration of the civilian economy. Tied up in an enormously expensive arms competition with the USSR, the United States has lost status and competitiveness in the commercial market. Significantly, the United States and the USSR, first in the capacity to wreak military destructiveness (as distinguished from first in the capacity to exercise *power*) rank, respectively, 7 and 23 among 141 nations in economic-social standing.[17]

National security means far more than the capacity for military destructiveness. Indeed the frenzied search for sustaining and expanding this capacity has produced a continuing erosion of those elements that account for real power in world affairs. By accelerating its commitment to military priorities at the expense of social and economic needs, this country has retarded its economic development through inflation, diversion of investment, misuse of scarce materials, and misuse of human capital. Small wonder then that in a recent article dealing with the implications of Reagan administration economies for the nation's universities, the president of Columbia University spoke of disquieting developments wherein "the per capita gross national product of the United States has slipped to tenth place in the world" and "our foreign trade pattern resembles that of an underdeveloped country."[18]

Largely because of the consequences of its enormous commitment to military spending, the United States now exports raw materials in abundance and imports more manufactured goods than it sells abroad. In striking relation to its robust expansion of military spending, the United States has created a distinct government-dependent civilian sector inherently prone to inflation. Inflation and waste result from its practice of rapid obsolescence and frequent product change, as well as from unstable markets, the excessive waste characteristic of large bureaucracies beyond public control, cost-plus pricing, and reduced management efficiency. Instead of being a major instrument for stimulating productivity, competitiveness, and innovation, our commitment to research has produced widespread recession and a society less and less able to provide its citizens with improved conditions of living. Among ten developed nations over the past twenty years, the slowest growth in investment and manufacturing productivity has occurred in the United States and the United Kingdom, where military expenditures have been the highest in relation to gross national product (GNP). The best investment and productivity record has been in Japan, where the military-to-GNP ratio has been very low and where productivity has grown at 8 percent per year.[19]

What exactly does heavy military spending do to undermine our economic and social stability? The answer is straightforward and widely understood by economists, although it has yet to be widely appreciated by the general public.

Most obviously, perhaps, heavy military spending generates a stream of buying power without producing an equivalent supply of economically useful goods for the civilian market. The excess of disposable income over available supply builds up a steady and generalized pressure on prices. As recent experience suggests, this excess becomes a prescription for permanent and corrosive inflation. The problem is exacerbated by the fact that military demand also adds directly to the pressure on prices for specific goods, especially when military purchases are directed to the commodities and labor skills in shortest supply.

Heavy military spending also preempts resources that might have been otherwise invested. While an enormous share of available public funds go to weapons, the United States ignores essential research that could develop new sources of energy, increase food production, provide better housing, and improve health, employment, and all around human well-being. These distorted priorities perpetually limit innovation and investment, thus occasioning national insecurity through low growth and slow productivity gains.

Military spending, especially at such inordinately high levels, is a profound burden on the economy, not a stimulant. When it is authorized at levels that vastly exceed legitimate security needs, it wastes irreplaceable resources, aggravates inflation, retards the production of consumer goods, and impairs sound economic growth. It follows, in the words of a report from the Center for Defense Information, that

> The top priority for U.S. political leadership is to foster and insure an *economic security* that is not dependent on big military budgets. When enough jobs can be created and sustained by the civilian economy, the only consideration for determining military expenditures will once again be our real need for armaments, and the Pentagon budget will no longer be used as an escape from the real economic problems facing the nation.[20]

The American commitment to militarization has also resulted in a steadily diminishing contribution to foreign aid for other countries. And what sort of world is it that we turn our backs on? Consider the following:

870 million adults cannot read and write
500 million people have no jobs or are underemployed
130 million children are unable to attend primary school
450 million people suffer from hunger and malnutrition
12 million babies die every year before their first birthday
42 million people are blind
1 billion people do not have safe drinking water
250 million people live in urban slums or shantytowns.[21]

It should not be assumed, however, that our unconcern for these unmet human needs is simply a form of well-reasoned (albeit callous) *realpolitik*. Rather, it is strikingly unrealistic, even in orthodox geopolitical terms, since worldwide human decay will foster a steadily rising spiral of violence and repression, a spiral that will inevitably heighten the probability for superpower confrontations and international war.

True national security requires a thoughtful balance between economic and military power and a prior understanding that the latter is not always advanced by the acquisition of expanded forces of destructiveness. To exercise a genuinely decisive influence in world affairs, the United States will need to emphasize the revitalization of its economy. And this, in turn, will require a progressive disengagement from debilitating patterns of military spending. In the words of the Washington-based Committee for National Security:

> As a nation, America needs to make a more realistic evaluation of its power. Military forces must not be designed for missions they cannot carry out, and policies must not be limited to narrow military responses. The national security debate must not ignore the non-military challenges to national security. These challenges must be taken as seriously as military threats. Now, more than ever, our nation must develop political, economic, social and diplomatic strategies to promote our vital interests.[22]

Notes

1. See "1980 Review Conference of the Treaty on the Non-Proliferation of Nuclear Weapons," ACDA Special Report, November 1980, 14 pp.
2. "Reagan's Statement on Nuclear Weapons," *The New York Times*, July 17, 1981, p. 6.
3. Paul Warnke, "Arms Control: A Global Imperative," *The Bulletin of the Atomic Scientists* 34, no. 6 (June 1978): 33–34.
4. "Arming for Arms Control," *The New York Times*, July 17, 1981, p. 20.

5. "On Nuclear War," *The New York Review of Books* 28, nos. 21 and 22, January 21, 1982, p. 10.

6. Barnet, *Real Security: Restoring American Power in a Dangerous Decade*. (New York: Simon and Schuster, 1981), p. 18.

7. Taken from Ruth Leger Sivard, *World Military and Social Expenditures 1981*, World Priorities, Leesburg, Va., p. 14.

8. Testimony to Committee of November 9, 1981, on "Strategic Weapons Proposals," p. 141.

9. *Fiscal Year 1982 Arms Control Impact Statements*, p. viii.

10. "The Anti-Ballistic Missile Treaty and National Security," Committee for National Security, CNS Issue Brief I, September 4, 1981. Reprinted with permission.

11. *An Arms Control Agenda for the Eighties*, Committee for National Security, Washington, D.C., June 30, 1981, p. 10. (I am one of the authors of the CNS report.)

12. At this time, research is also being conducted on such exotic ASAT weapons as high-energy lasers and charged particle beam weapons. Largely under the auspices of the Defense Advanced Research Projects Agency (DARPA), these programs are underway to threaten further the warning and communications satellites of adversary forces. It follows that such programs will increase each side's fear of surprise attack by the other, adding to instability in nuclear deterrence. For more information on these developments, see "Preparing for Nuclear War: President Reagan's Program," *The Defense Monitor* 10, no. 8 (1982):16 pp.

13. In this connection, a clear difference in priorities is evident between the Carter and Reagan administrations. The difference is elucidated by a comparison of the positions of former secretaries of state Muskie and Haig. Speaking before the Senate foreign relations committee on September 16, 1980, on "U.S. Nuclear Strategy," Muskie emphasized that "American nuclear strategy should be fully consistent with our arms control objectives, so that we preserve the opportunities to strengthen security and stability by means of equitable and verifiable arms control agreements" (U.S. Department of State, Bureau of Public Affairs, *Current Policy*, no. 219, p. 1). More recently, in an address before the Foreign Policy Association in New York on July 14, 1981, Secretary Haig stated,

> arms control can only be one element in a comprehensive structure of defense and foreign policy designed to reduce the risks of war. It cannot be the political centerpiece or the crucial barometer of U.S.-Soviet relationships . . . Arms control proposals should be designed in the context of the security situation we face, our military needs, and our defense strategy. Arms control should complement military programs in meeting these needs.

(U.S. Department of State, Bureau of Public Affairs, "Arms Control for the 1980's: An American Policy," *Current Policy*, no. 292, p. 2.)

14. From Sivard, *World Military and Social Expenditures 1981*, p. 13.

15. Kennan's "On Nuclear War," p. 10.

16. Herbert York, *Race to Oblivion: A Participant's View of the Arms Race* (New York: Simon and Schuster, 1970), pp. 230–31.

17. Sivard, *World Military and Social Expenditures 1981*, p. 5.

18. Michael I. Sovern, "The Case for Keeping U.S. Aid to Colleges," *The New York Times Magazine*, February 7, 1982, p. 75.

19. Sivard, *World Military and Social Expenditures 1981*, p. 19.

20. "Jobs and the Pentagon: Is Military Spending Good for the Economy," *The Defense Monitor* 6, no. 7 (September-October 1977):8.

21. See Sivard, *World Military and Social Expenditures 1981*, p. 20.

22. See "Statement of Purpose," Committee for National Security, Washington, D.C.

6 The Future of Nuclear Deterrence

The fifth major assumption of current American nuclear strategy is that peace can be maintained indefinitely via nuclear deterrence. Lacking any insightful plan for more enduring world order reform, this strategy is content with perpetuating a system of deadly logic that cannot possibly last out the century. At one time or another, in one way or another, the manifestly catastrophic possibilities that now lie latent in nuclear weapons are almost certain to be exploited, either by design or by accident, by misinformation or miscalculation, by lapse from rational decision or by unauthorized decision.

Despite the success of nuclear deterrence thus far, a nuclear war between the superpowers could come to pass in several ways.[1] It might come about inadvertently through the outcome of competition in risk taking. It might begin by the seizure of nuclear weapons by allied countries. It might be provoked by a smaller power or by war between smaller powers.

Or it might take place because of errors in calculating the outcomes of various anticipated courses of action. It might even take place as a consequence of irrationality, through use by unauthorized personnel, or by mechanical, electrical, or computer malfunction. This last possibility is especially disturbing. Consider the following scenario:

> It is a routine day for the personnel who man the command and control systems for this country's nuclear forces. An integral part of the U.S. Worldwide Military Command and Control System (WWMCCS), these systems function to assure communications between the National Command Authority (the president and the secretary of defense), the joint chiefs of staff, and nuclear forces in the field. Suddenly officers at the North American Air Defense Command (NORAD) at Colorado Springs receive information that the United States is under attack from Soviet submarine-launched nuclear missiles. Responding to the sensing system that has provided the early warning, ten jet intercepters from bases in the United States and Canada are scrambled aloft, and missile bases throughout the nation are placed on low-level alert. Only one minute before the information is transmitted to President Reagan and Secretary of Defense Weinberger, however, a mechanical error is discovered. The alert is a false alarm, set off when a "war game" tape was mistakenly loaded into a NORAD computer and read as a "live launch."

The events described in this scenario are not fiction. They have already taken place, not once, but many times during the past several years. After one of these occasions, on November 9, 1979, the official Soviet press agency, Tass, criticized the error and warned that another such episode could have "irreparable consequences for the whole world."[2]

The Soviets may have good reason to be concerned. Consider the following record of recent mishaps[3]:

> Over a recent 18-month period the U.S. nuclear warning system produced 147 false indications of Soviet missile attacks.
>
> The U.S. government reactor in South Carolina that produces plutonium and tritium for nuclear warheads has had a steady increase in incidents with nuclear hazard potential. In 1975 38 incidents were recorded; by 1980 there were 108 incidents in the year. None was publicly announced.
>
> In 1980 a wrench accidentally dropped by a technician punctured a Titan II missile, igniting and exploding the leaking fuel. The blast blew a 750-ton cover off the silo and created a fireball visible for 30 miles.
>
> The Hanford Nuclear Reservation, 200 miles from Seattle, Washington, has had 20 leaks, totaling 435,000 gallons of liquid radioactive materials, in the last 10 years. Hanford is the largest of the nation's nuclear waste disposal sites.
>
> At SAC headquarters in Nebraska, 39 airmen, including some who had access to sensitive information, were arrested on suspicion of selling or using drugs on the base.
>
> Between 1950 and 1980 the Department of Defense recorded 32 accidents involving its nuclear weapons. There were no nuclear detonations, but two accidents, one in Spain and a second in Greenland, resulted in widespread dispersion of nuclear materials.
>
> A power dip at the North American Air Defense Command in Colorado put out of commission for an hour the computers that monitor radar and warn of an enemy air attack.
>
> In Florida a robot being tested to operate a nuclear reactor went berserk, ripping its shoulder off and beating itself into scrap metal.
>
> A U.S. navy submarine accidentally launched a live but nonnuclear missile in the direction of the Caribbean island of St. Croix. While the search was on, the official navy spokesman said, "We have our fingers crossed that it landed in the sea."

Recent pentagon tests of its multibillion dollar world wide military command and control system—the computer nerve center of the entire United States military apparatus—indicate serious shortcomings. A test of

WWMCCS in spring 1977, called Prime Target, linked up computers in the U.S. Atlantic Command (LANTCOM), European Command (EUCOM), Readiness Command (REDCOM), Tactical Air Command (TAC), and the National Military Command Center. Overall, the computers failed 62 percent of the time.[4]

It should not be assumed, however, that only the United States is subject to false warnings and communications failures that might lead to nuclear war. The Soviets, too, depend upon highly complex warning systems and command and control systems that are subject to failure. And it is very likely that their systems have experienced the same sorts of breakdowns over the years as our own. The difference is that we do not learn of their problems in the newspapers.

To get an idea of the number and complexity of strategic warning and control systems, consider the following information from SAC headquarters[5]: The United States relies on early warning satellite systems and the ballistic missile early warning system (BMEWS) radars for indication of ICBM attacks. For warning of submarine launched ballistic missile (SLBM) attacks, we rely upon satellites and detection and warning system radars, the latter eventually to be replaced with newer phased-array radars. The U.S. Air Force Strategic Air Command (SAC), this country's primary nuclear deterrent force, is designed to receive the weapons expenditure authority, or "go code," via the joint chiefs of staff (JCS) alerting network. Perhaps the most important of all SAC-owned communications systems is the primary alerting system (PAS), which employs the famous red telephone. This voice communication system, designed for alert and launch of SAC forces, would reach each SAC unit via two widely separated routes.

Together with voice systems SAC uses digital transmission media to provide the printed word to command and control elements of the force. A medium-power, high-frequency, single-sideband radio system (ALFA NET) provides the means for positive control of the SAC airborne force. But because high-frequency radio is not always dependable in the Arctic regions, the high-power, single-sideband system is supplemented by an ultra-high-frequency system known as Green Pine. Additionally there exists a survivable low-frequency communications system (SLFCS) and a post-attack command control system (PACCS). The latter system is best known for its SAC airborne command post (ABNCP), modified 747B jet transports (E4), which are continuously airborne near headquarters in Nebraska, maintaining voice and data communication links with SAC and U.S. Air Force command control facilities worldwide.

The idea that a nuclear war might begin by accident has been with us for some time. In the popular novel and movie *Fail Safe* an American nuclear attack on the USSR is triggered by a statistically impossible double mechanical failure that sends this country's bombers to Moscow. The story plays fast and loose with the actual facts of American command and control; nonetheless it does point correctly to the inherent and unavoidable risks involved in mechanical and electronic systems, risks that may be heightened rather than lowered by the piling of one system upon another. (At least one NORAD false warning was allegedly set off by the deterioration of a 47 cent computer chip.)

The malfunction of nuclear weapon systems must also be considered from the standpoint of nuclear weapon accidents which, although they have no bearing upon the problem of accidental nuclear war between the superpowers, may nonetheless have catastrophic effects. One must look at the American record of accidents involving nuclear weapons, at least as far as that record is known. According to the Department of Defense:

> There has been a total of 33 accidents involving US nuclear weapons throughout the period that the US has had these weapons. Because of the inherent safety features, the control features, the administrative procedures designed into US nuclear weapon systems and the precautions taken during operations with these weapons, there has never been a case where a nuclear detonation had occurred in a nuclear weapon accident.[6]

According to the Center for Defense Information, however, evidence exists of many other nuclear weapon accidents that have gone unreported or unconfirmed. In the words of the Center publication, *The Defense Monitor*, "Serious students of the problem estimate that an average of one U.S. nuclear accident has occurred every year since 1945, with some estimating as many as thirty major nuclear accidents and 250 'minor' nuclear accidents during that time."[7]

Yet this does not suggest that each of the superpowers is failing to take precautions against the accidental use of nuclear weapons. While very little is known about the USSR in this regard, the U.S. safety program comprises four basic standards required for all nuclear weapon systems. According to the Department of Defense, these standards are as follows:

1. There shall be positive measures to prevent nuclear weapons involved in accidents or incidents or jettisoned weapons from producing a nuclear yield.
2. There shall be positive measures to prevent DELIBERATE prearming, arming, launching, firing, or releasing of nuclear weapons, except upon execution of emergency war orders or when directed by competent authority.
3. There shall be positive measures to prevent INADVERTENT prearming, arming, launching, firing, or releasing of nuclear weapons.
4. There shall be positive measures to insure adequate security of nuclear weapons, pursuant to the provisions of DOD Directive 5210.41.[8]

Following these standards, specified safety rules govern all nuclear weapon system operations in which the nuclear weapon is vulnerable to being inadvertently launched, prearmed, armed, fired, detonated, released, or lost. The scope of these safety rules is identified in a Department of Defense directive as follows:

> Safety Rules shall include general provisions applicable to all nuclear weapon operations throughout the stockpile-to-target sequence (storage, maintenance, handling, transportation, delivery, etc.) and specific provisions to provide adequate safety for unique nuclear weapon system operations (alerts, operational posturing, maneuvers, exercises, training, etc.).[9]

The principal steps taken to avert accidental use of nuclear weapons by American forces include strict custodial control of these weapons and a considerable array of redundant safety features. These features are incorporated into the chain of command and into the weapons themselves. Where they concern the chain of command, these features are highlighted by the so-called two-man concept, whereby no single individual has the ability to fire nuclear weapons; by a control system whereby each individual with a nuclear weapons responsibility has been formally certified under the "human reliability program"; and by the use of "secure codes."

Where they concern the weapons themselves, these features emphasize "highly secure coded locking devices." Moreover, although the exact release procedures for nuclear weapons are highly classified, it is known that safeguards against accidental nuclear firings do vary somewhat from one weapon system to another.

While the weapons engineers and the military authorities must be commended for the fact that none of the nuclear weapon accidents has produced a nuclear explosion, it would be foolish to assume that we can avoid accidental nuclear war or nuclear weapon accidents indefinitely. And this is to say nothing of the Soviet system of positive control or the Soviet system of safeguards about which we know so little.

For example, exactly how strict and how reliable is the Soviet system of codes and communications? What sorts of safety devices are built into the Soviet weapons themselves? What kind of "human reliability program" is operative among Soviet personnel who deal with nuclear weapons? What sorts of redundancies are built into Soviet command and control procedures for nuclear weapons expenditure? Do these procedures include an alternate national military command center as well as a network of airborne command posts to provide reliability? What is the Soviet safety record concerning accidents involving nuclear weapons?

The threat of accidental nuclear war between the United States and the USSR is aggravated by the command and control systems of other nuclear powers, both those systems already in existence (especially China and India) and those systems of countries soon to join the nuclear club. Since other nuclear powers will have great difficulty in protecting their nuclear forces from first-strike attack, they will almost certainly turn to the deployment of nuclear weapons provided with automatic systems of nuclear retaliation (based upon the processing of electronic warnings by computer) and to the pre-delegation of launch authority. The resultant conditions are certain to pose grave hazards to everyone.

The spread of such conditions would affect the likelihood of nuclear war between the United States and the USSR for at least two reasons: First, the generally greater likelihood of nuclear war associated with relaxed command and control over nuclear weapons implies a general increase in the number of conflicts that might involve superpower participation. This is especially true if the initial nuclear conflict were to involve an ally of one or both of the superpowers. Second, with the steady increase in the number of nuclear powers, it is conceivable that a new nuclear power could launch its nuclear weapons against one or the other superpowers without the victim knowing for certain where the attack originated. In the event that the victim were to conclude that the attack came from the other superpower, a full-scale nuclear war between the United States and the USSR might ensue. In such a case the new nuclear power, possibly as a result of its own inadequate system of command and control, will have catalyzed nuclear war between the superpowers.

Regrettably little can be done about the flaws in the systems of command and control of nuclear weapons. The essential fault lies not with these systems but in the underlying strategy of peace through nuclear deterrence. The implementation of even more stringent measures to prevent the accidental use of nuclear weapons would in most cases impair the credibility of a country's nuclear deterrence position. As long as nations continue to base their hopes for peace and security on the ability to deliver overwhelming nuclear destruction to an aggressor, the risk of accidental nuclear war and of other nuclear weapon accidents will simply have to be endured.

The ingredients of a credible deterrence posture are exceedingly complex. Such a posture requires a state to successfully persuade would be aggressors that it possesses the ability and the resolve to respond with unacceptably damaging retaliation. This is no mean feat. In terms of ability, it means being judged capable of withstanding a first-strike attack and of penetrating the would be attacker's active defenses with unacceptable levels of destruction. In terms of resolve, it means being judged willing actually to deliver the promised repraisal. There is little reason to believe that all states are likely to meet these requirements even in the short run, let alone indefinitely.

Moreover the presumed rationality upon which deterrence rests is itself very doubtful. The actual behavior of national decisionmakers is obviously not always rational. And even if we could believe that their behavior is always rational, this would say nothing about the accuracy of the information used in rational calculations. Rationality refers only to the *intention* of maximizing specified values or preferences. It does not tell us anything about whether the information used is correct or incorrect. Hence rational actors may make errors in calculation that lead them to nuclear war and destruction.

It is also worth noting that the ability to make rational decisions in world politics is frequently undercut by the consequences of crisis and stress. Even national leaders who deliberately gear their decisions toward the preservation of the state may actually precipitate contrary effects. This might be the result of errors in information or faulty calculations engendered by stress-warping of perception and alertness. In the post-Watergate era in American politics, one can only speculate how close a president of the United States may already have come to experiencing the level of emotional strain required to upset rational decisionmaking in world politics.

The myth that nuclear deterrence can work indefinitely between the superpowers also contributes to the proliferation of nuclear weapons to other countries. Consequently as long as this myth is sustained by current American nuclear strategy, this country's security will be further eroded by the additional dangers of nuclear weapons spread. By failing to live up to the requirements of article 6 of the nuclear nonproliferation treaty, the United States will encourage the appearance of new nuclear weapons states that will quickly engage in qualitative and quantitative nuclear arms races of their own. The net effect of such arms races can only be a greatly heightened risk of nuclear war, for the superpowers and for every other state. Consider the following:

> The expanded number of nuclear powers would weaken the idea of a stable balance of terror in world politics. There would simply be too many players, too much ambiguity, for any sense of balance to be meaningful.
>
> The expanded number of nuclear powers would further shatter the symmetry of strategic doctrine between nuclear weapons states. Some of the new nuclear powers would shape their strategies along the lines of minimum deterrence or assured destruction. Others would seek more ambitious objectives, including a nuclear war-fighting or counterforce capability. As a result nuclear weapons might quickly lose their already precarious image as instruments of deterrence, a situation that would surely be accelerated by the first actual use of nuclear weapons by a secondary nuclear power. If for example the nuclear firebreak were crossed in the Middle East late in this decade, whether by Israel or by an Arab state, other pairs of antagonistic states would be more likely to

think the unthinkable. A ripple effect would begin to be evident, with perhaps Libya contemplating preemption against Egypt or Iran thinking seriously about a nuclear strike against Iraq.

The expanded number of nuclear powers would ultimately create the conditions whereby first-strike attacks could be unleashed with impunity, whatever the condition of the intended victim's willingness to retaliate or the security of its retaliatory forces. This is the case because in a world of many nuclear powers, it would become possible for a nuclear-armed aggressor to launch its weapons against another state without being identified. Unable to know for certain where the attack originated, the victim state might lash out blindly. In the resulting conflagration, a worldwide nuclear war enveloping even the superpowers might ensue.

The expanded number of nuclear powers would create the conditions for a chain reaction of nuclear exchanges. Even before it becomes possible to launch a nuclear strike anonymously, a strategic exchange might take place between two or more new nuclear weapons states that are members of opposing alliances. Ultimately if the parties to such a clash involve clients of either or both superpowers, the ensuing chain reaction might consume the United States and the USSR along with much of the rest of the world.

The expanded number of nuclear powers would create the conditions whereby microproliferation—the spread of nuclear weapons capabilities to insurgent groups—might be accelerated. A possible outcome of such microproliferation might be not only nuclear terrorism, but also an anonymous terrorist detonation that could be mistakenly blamed upon another state by the attack victim. In this way microproliferation could actually spark regional or systemwide nuclear war between states.

The expanded number of nuclear weapons would create major asymmetries in power between rival states. Where one rival would find itself in possession of nuclear weapons and another rival would be denied such possession, the new nuclear state might find itself with an overwhelming incentive to strike. The cumulative effect of such inequalities of power created by the uneven spread of nuclear weapons would be an elevated probability of nuclear aggression against non-nuclear states.

Perhaps the greatest hazard involved in the expanded number of nuclear powers is one that has been suggested not by a professional strategist but by the distinguished Swiss playright and novelist, Max Frisch, in his work, *The Great Wall of China*:

> Whoever sits on a throne today has mankind in his hand, its whole history, beginning with Moses or Buddha, including the Acropolis, the temples of the Mayas, the Gothic cathedrals, including the whole of Western philosophy, French and Spanish painting, German music, Shakespeare, including this young couple, Romeo and Juliet. And including all of us, our children, our children's children. A passing mood on the part of anyone who sits on a throne today, a nervous breakdown, a neurosis, a flash of megalomania, a moment of impatience brought on by indigestion, and everything will be done for. Every thing! A cloud of yellow or brown ashes towering up to the sky, looking like a mushroom, like a dirty cauliflower, and the rest is silence—radioactive silence.

These remarks reveal the most insidious aspect of nuclear proliferation: its bestowal, upon a tiny number of unsteady national leaders, of apocalyptic potentiality. Whereas in the past the defects of human personality among heads of state have wreaked terrible consequences, in the future these defects may give rise to oblivion. Combined with a spreading nuclear weapons capability, the vagaries of life on a throne portend a global inferno beyond even Dante's power of description.

We already know about the probable consequences of nuclear war, consequences that call forth an almost hallucinatory specter of congealed evil. The march of nations eager to join the nuclear club is leading the species to a lemming-like extinction. Unless it is halted while there is still time, this march will defile even the least trodden sanctuaries. Unless it is turned about before the final ascent of witlessness, few of our paralyzed desiccated voices will be left to wail funereally.

The consequences of a nuclear war occurring through proliferation call forth an entirely new paradigm of death. Born of our species' most twisted technological accomplishments, this paradigm expands our scope of apocalyptic symbolization to new dimensions. With such a paradigm we can begin to fashion a framework for interpreting and absorbing the vision of worldwide nuclear obliteration, a constellation of concepts and images that allows us to comprehend not only gigadeath (death in the billions) but the final triumph of meaninglessness and discontinuity. We need such a framework because with the proliferation of nuclear weapons the consequences of nuclear war could be effectively boundless.

The consequences of a nuclear war resulting from proliferation need not necessarily signal worldwide devastation. While the spread of nuclear weapons makes such devastation much more probable, it also creates new arenas for local or regional nuclear conflict. What might happen in these new arenas therefore must be treated as one set of consequences of nuclear war resulting from proliferation.

Indeed in appraising the effects of nuclear war that might arise from proliferation, the reader must examine the spectrum of nuclear conflict possibilities. What exactly would be the consequences of a nuclear war arising from such possibilities? Would the world be transformed into an enormous necropolis, a world city of the dead? Would a dreadful pall descend over the planet, entombing the dead and the dying together in a blasted and surrealistic scene strewn with fragments of bodies and imaginations?

Or would we be spared so sweeping an agony? Would the full horror of butchered lives and broken dreams be localized, sparing the innocent bystanders of noncombatant countries? Could we expect only a limited hell as the price of a limited nuclear war?

And what exactly would such a hell reveal? Dante's hell had a definite and unambiguous shape. It was a huge funnel ringed with tormented sinners, far, far away from the celestial throne. The hell on earth that would be produced by nuclear war between the superpowers has the terrible anonymity of Kafka's castle. Of course, we can supply reams of facts, tables, and charts to lend substance to what appears to lie ahead, but such information can never satisfactorily dispel the fearful knowledge that we really do not *know*, that we really cannot *feel*, the measureless dread and deprivation that would be experienced by the survivors. This incapacity for a genuine experiential link to survivors of a nuclear war is merely an extension of a more basic incapacity, the inability of human beings to imagine their own deaths.

The phenomenon of standing outside the arena of mortality, of denying that our individual organisms must sooner or later submit to total annihilation, does even more than obstruct real empathy and understanding. It produces one of the most dangerous barriers to preventing nuclear war. Even the most horrible visions of massive nuclear violation will prove insufficient cause for prophylactic measures among populations that cannot really picture themselves as victims. The irony of this condition in a world suffused with literary, artistic, and political imageries of extinction is overwhelming.

If the proliferation of nuclear weapons should lead to a nuclear war involving the exchange of 1 million megatons of nuclear explosives, the world would probably experience what Nevil Shute described in his modern classic, *On the Beach*. Assuming a global irradiation of around 500 rad, those who do not succumb to the effects of blast and heat would survive no longer than a few weeks. Dwarfing even the horrendous calamity postulated in the National Academy of Sciences Report, *Long-Term Worldwide Effects of Multiple Nuclear-Weapons Detonations*, such a war would represent humankind's last and most complete holocaust, defying not only our imaginations of disaster but our customary measurements as well. Worldwide nuclear war would represent not only unprecedented virtuosity in killing power but the final disappearance of the very boundaries of annihilation.

A worldwide nuclear war would occasion no problems of survivor guilt, no long-term physical or mental scars, no profound feelings of death-in-life. In the aftermath of such a war there would be no advantage for populations that had burrowed themselves into fallout shelters or had dutifully relocated themselves in "safe" areas. No benefits would accrue to those citizens who had heeded their government's warning to carry credit cards and sanitary napkins into relocation centers. In the United States members of the reservist government would be unmoved by the commitment to place them on the federal payroll during the time of crisis. Even in the USSR the all important cadres would fail to draw life-giving support from the system that sought to assure their survival.

While, as Robert Jay Lifton has said, to "touch death" and then rejoin the living can be a vital source of insight and power, a worldwide nuclear war would deprive us of this source.[10] By killing even time and memory, such a war would imply that survivors could never be mentors to the world. Although the vision of total annihilation must now be cultivated for the life-sustaining forms it might still help to create, the fulfillment of that vision would forever block all hope and revitalization. Our own Protean possibilities, our capacity for adapting shape to situation, demand the understanding that the outer limits of lethal conflict are final and remorseless.

Ironically, if there should be a nuclear war, it would almost certainly *not* be because of evil motives or malevolence. The impending spread of nuclear weapons is fueled not by madness or base purpose, but by basically well-intentioned people who find such weapons essential to "national security." The tilt toward nuclear war is not an ineradicable aspect of humankind's biological endowment, an affliction of the germ plasm to be endured with resignation. Rather, it is the product of *thoughtlessness*, the literal inability to understand the probable outcome of complex strategic interactions. In the words of Albert Camus, "What strikes me, in the midst of polemics, threats and outbursts of violence, is the fundamental good will of everyone."[11]

Notes

1. In this connection success is defined very narrowly in terms of the avoidance of nuclear war. Where the workings of nuclear deterrence are considered more broadly in terms of effects on day-to-day life under the threat of nuclear annihilation, however, they can hardly be termed a success. For example the prevailing system of deadly logic has had terribly corrosive effects on ordinary human feelings of care and compassion. In the United States small but growing bands of Americans dubbed "survivalists"

are arming themselves and learning how to kill in a postapocalypse milieu. Going far beyond the self-help aspect of the bomb shelter movement of the 1950s and 1960s, this retreat to medieval thinking entails a heightened form of social-darwinism, a generally accepted willingness to kill neighbors to survive. As one survivalist in northern Georgia put it recently, "If there is a nuclear war, I hope everyone in the cities is killed. I don't want them coming out afterwards expecting me to feed them or to take what I've got."

Another frequently overlooked cost of nuclear deterrence is the accumulation of vast quantities of nuclear waste. Up till now, 99 percent by volume of all high-level nuclear wastes (the most radioactive) in the United States has come from military activities. Since nuclear wastes can be dangerous to human beings not only through direct contact but also by getting into water supplies or the food chain of plants and animals that we eat, this cost of nuclear deterrence cannot be taken lightly. Indeed even if all nuclear reactors were shut down today and not another hydrogen bomb produced, we would still have a mountain of nuclear wastes that could seriously imperil future generations. (See "Military Nuclear Wastes: The Hidden Burden of the Nuclear Arms Race," *The Defense Monitor*) 10, no. 1 (1981).

A far more widely understood cost of nuclear deterrence is, of course, the economic deterioration and social unrest brought by steadily rising military expenditures. As we have already seen, military spending is uniquely inflationary. Although the Reagan administration's budget cuts are intended to create expectations of success in fighting inflation, its expanded military spending will overheat the ecomony by generating more spendable income than goods and services to absorb it. This spending will also have a depressing effect on investment, which will in turn thwart economic growth and prolong inflationary pressures.

In the final analysis the essential human costs of military spending associated with the dead-end search for protracted nuclear deterrence are vast unmet needs for income, education, health, nutrition, and housing. In the words of the distinguished economist, Ruth Leger Sivard, "In short, what the arms race means in human terms is that more people are condemned to die of hunger and of foul water; children to grow up retarded in body and mind; the special needs of the elderly to be neglected; people to live out their lives in fear and with hate" (*World Military and Social Expenditures 1980*, World Priorities, Leesburg, Va., 1980, p. 18). For more information on the debilitating economic effects of the arms race, see John Kenneth Galbraith, "The Economics of the Arms Race—and After," *East/West Outlook* 4, no. 2 (May-June 1981); Admiral Gene R. LaRocque, "We Spend Too Much on Defense," *The New York Times*, February 1, 1981, p. F3; Wassily Leontief, "Big Boosts in Defense Risk 'Economic Calamity,'" an interview with the Nobel Prize-winning economist in *U.S. News and World Report*, 1981, reprinted by the Committee for National Security; and

Seymour Melman, "Beating 'Swords' into Subways," *The New York Times Magazine*, November 19, 1978, p. 43.

2. The 1980 Titan missile accident in the United States can hardly have been reassuring to the Soviets.

3. From *World Military and Social Expenditures 1981* by Ruth Leger Sivard. Leesburg, Virginia: World Priorities, p. 15, ©World Priorities, Leesburg, Va. 22075. Reprinted with permission.

4. See my article prepared for the Independent News Alliance (INA) in July 1980, "Flaws in Systems of Command and Control: Nuclear War by Accident."

5. SAC, *Information*, Offutt Air Force Base, n.d.

6. From U.S. Department of Defense undated press release sent to me on June 16, 1976, by U.S. Air Force Lieutenant General W.Y. Smith assistant to the chairman of the joint chiefs of staff.

7. *The Defense Monitor* 4, no.2 (February 1975):9.

8. *Safety Studies and Reviews of Nuclear Weapons Systems*, U.S. Department of Defense Directive no. 5030.15, August 8, 1974, pp. 3–4.

9. Ibid., p. 2.

10. Lifton, *The Life of the Self: Toward a New Psychology* (New York: Simon and Schuster, 1976), p. 115.

11. Albert Camus, *Neither Victims nor Executioners* (New York: Continuum, 1980), p. 31. *Neither Victims nor Executioners* first appeared serially in the fall 1946 issues of *Combat*, the newspaper of the French Resistance that Camus helped to edit during the Nazi occupation and for a short time after the war. The translation is by Dwight MacDonald.

7 Solutions

Since the primary arena of nuclear-war avoidance is *intra*national, reversing America's current nuclear strategy will require a rapid and far-reaching disengagement from developing patterns of counterforce targeting and from expanding preparations for nuclear war fighting. Only when such disengagement is complete can a viable arms-control agenda be implemented. Hence only in the aftermath of such disengagement can we expect genuine movement to an improved world order.

To accomplish the necessary revisions in American nuclear strategy, the U.S. government must move immediately to restore the relatively promising principles of minimum deterrence. The overriding objective of such a move must be to reduce Soviet fears of an American first strike while preserving the survivability and penetration capability of this country's strategic forces. This objective can be served by abandoning plans for additional deployment of nuclear weapons for hard-target kills; abandoning plans for any ICBM basing mode that assumes deployment of a ballistic missile defense system; abandoning plans for civil defense and crisis relocation of civilian populations; and abandoning provocative plans for stepped-up decapitation attacks on Soviet command, control, communication and intelligence (C^3I) facilities.[1]

With such stabilizing moves underway, the superpowers could begin to make progress toward a START accord, which in turn would allow for successful limitations on long-range theater nuclear forces in Europe and on antisatellite weapons systems. Moreover the realization of a START agreement would further the objectives of the limited test ban treaty and the nuclear nonproliferation treaty.

The ultimate objective of START must be an agreement wherein both sides undertake substantial reductions in strategic forces. Before this objective can be realized, moves toward minimum deterrence must be augmented by a comprehensive test ban (CTB) treaty, by American renunciation of the right to first use of nuclear weapons, by the implementation of a U.S.–Soviet nuclear weapons freeze, and by the progressive implementation of additional zones free of nuclear weapons.

Comprehensive Test Ban

Only a comprehensive test ban can genuinely inhibit further nuclear weapons innovations. A goal first outlined in the late 1950s, CTB should include all nuclear weapons states and the largest possible number of nonnuclear weapons states. However, even if France and China initially chose to remain outside such an agreement (neither France nor China has ratified the Partial Test Ban Treaty of 1963), CTB's prospective benefits are apt to be considerable enough to warrant endorsement. Understood in terms of the superpower responsibility to make avoidance of nuclear war credible in a world of self-assertive states, CTB could offer a critical starting point for wider imitation and reciprocity. Consider the following facts.[2]

Comprehensive Test Ban

The ban would prohibit all nuclear explosions in all environments.

Trilateral negotiations have been underway since 1977 between the United States, the USSR, and Great Britain.

Agreed upon treaty items thus far are

- fixed duration;
- moratorium on peaceful nuclear explosions for duration of treaty;
- on-site inspections and placement of specially equipped, tamper-proof seismic stations on territories of parties;
- international exchange of seismic data;
- committee of experts to consider questions related to seismic data exchange.

Arguments for the ban are that it

- aids U.S. efforts to stop proliferation of nuclear weapons;
- inhibits further development of new weapons;
- provides new momentum for arms control negotiations;
- reduces nuclear pollution;
- releases human and financial resources for peaceful purposes.

Arguments against the ban are that it

- prevents improvements in warhead designs;
- prevents reliability testing of the existing nuclear weapons stockpile;
- cannot be adequately verified, especially at low yields;
- does not completely ban nuclear testing (absent France and China).

The treaty's status is as follows:

1977: Resolutions were introduced in both Senate and House of Representatives urging president to

- propose immediate suspension of underground nuclear explosions to continue so long as USSR abstains;
- propose a permanent treaty to ban all nuclear explosions.

1978: Reports to House armed services committee generally hostile to a CTB.

Report by Senator Dewey Bartlett to Senate armed services committee hostile to CTB.

Report by Senator Frank Church to Senate foreign relation committee very favorable to CTB.

Both superpowers have historically been on record in favor of a comprehensive test ban. Former President Carter made such a ban one of the primary objectives of his program for arms control and disarmament. Mr. Carter's thoughts on the CTB were announced before the United Nations on March 17, 1977, and again on October 4, 1977, when he told the General Assembly: "The time has come to end all explosions of nuclear devices, no matter what their claimed justification, peaceful or military."

It is, however, the American lack of distinction between peaceful and military explosions that upsets the Soviets. Although the Soviets have recently backed off from a firm desire not to prevent peaceful nuclear explosions, they are still interested in making some allowances for such explosions in the future. Mr. Brezhnev has announced Soviet willingness to accept a moratorium on peaceful nuclear explosions in conjunction with a treaty prohibiting nuclear weapon tests, but he has tied this moratorium to a fixed period of time and to a series of continuing negotiations on the issue. An additional problem in concluding a CTB centers on verification of compliance, but continuing improvements in seismic technology suggest that on-site inspections will become less important and that mutually acceptable procedures are well within the range of feasibility.

Properly regarded as "America's longest unfulfilled promise in the area of nuclear arms control,"[3] the CTB treaty would commit the parties to achieve the discontinuance of all test explosions of nuclear weapons for all time. By urging Senate ratification of two supporting agreements, the 1974 Threshold Test Ban Treaty and the 1976 Treaty on Underground Explosions for Peaceful Purposes, the Reagan administration would be in an improved position to resume negotiations on a comprehensive ban and consequently to begin plans toward genuine denuclearization.

These facts notwithstanding, President Reagan announced, in July 1982 that his administration will not resume CTB negotiations with the USSR. Although the trilateral test ban talks, suspended by President Carter in 1980, had ended on an optimistic note, President Reagan clearly felt compelled to subordinate the requirements of arms control to his program for "revitalizing" the American nuclear deterrent. Seeking to go ahead with tests on such weapons as the new Pershing II cruise missile (which exploded on its first test flight just as the president suspended CTB talks), the administration threw out nineteen years of bipartisan American support for a CTB treaty.

This move speaks volumes about the administration's sincerity concerning arms control negotiations in general. Since the signing in 1963 by

American, British, and Soviet negotiators of the Limited Test Ban Treaty, every U.S. president regardless of party actively sought an agreement that would also halt underground nuclear testing. And during this period the military arguments for continued testing were consistently rejected.

With its suspension of CTB negotiations, the Reagan administration also announced its plan to concentrate on what it regards as inadequate verification provisions of two treaties signed in the 1970s by the Nixon and Ford administrations, but never ratified by the Senate. The administration's apprehensions center on suspicions that the Soviets have violated these treaties' 150-kiloton limit on underground nuclear explosions. Should it be able to replace these apprehensions with the understanding that adequate verification procedures are now available, the administration might still be able to move ahead with CTB in the future. Consider the following facts.[4]

Threshold Test Ban Treaty

Limits underground U.S. and Soviet nuclear tests to 150 kilotons.

Limits underground nuclear weapons tests "to a minimum."

Promises continuing negotiations to achieve "cessation of all underground nuclear weapon tests."

Details technical data to be exchanged and limits weapons-testing to designated test sites.

Permits one or two slight breaches of 150-kiloton limit per year.

Is bilateral, signed by the United States and the USSR in 1974.

Arguments against the treaty are that it

- aids in verifying test yields through exchanging geological data, by (1) establishing correlations between stated yields and seismic signals and (2) improving assessments of yields based on seismic instrument measurements;
- constrains the USSR from further warhead development of its larger missiles;
- constitutes progress toward a comprehensive test ban;
- provides useful information regarding Soviet nuclear testing program;
- helps reestablish momentum of arms control;
- confirms that the United States is an international negotiator in good faith.

Arguments against the treaty are that it

- ignores current verification capabilities (detection between 1 and 10 kilotons), so the threshold is meaningless;
- continues discriminatory aspects of 1963 limited test ban treaty permitting testing only by nuclear weapon states;

considered by many nonnuclear weapon states as not responsive to disarmament obligations undertaken by the United States and USSR under the nonproliferation treaty.

provides no incentives for near-nuclear nations to refrain from their own testing programs;

weakens political support for a CTB;

treaties are bilateral, not multilateral.

The United States and the USSR abide by threshold aspect of treaty only.

Status of the treaty:

Executive: under review.

Legislative: hearings were held before Senate foreign relations committee in 1977; presently in committee.

Treaty on Underground Nuclear Explosions for Peaceful Purposes (PNET)

Governs all nuclear explosions at sites other than weapons test sites specified under threshold test ban treaty (TTBT).

Limits individual nuclear explosions to 150 kilotons, multiple explosions to 1,500 kilotons.

Establishes a joint consultative commission to discuss questions of compliance, develop on-site inspection processes, facilitate cooperation in PNE-related areas.

Links PNET and TTBT by forbidding termination of PNET while TTBT remains in force; stipulates simultaneous exchange of ratification instruments.

Details technical data to be exchanged; specifies when observers can inspect PNE preparations and install advanced instrumentation as well as the equipment they may bring and the functions they may perform.

Is bilateral, signed by the United States and the USSR in 1976.

Arguments for the treaty are that it

provides unprecedented on-site verification inspections including installation and operation of local seismic network, radio links for data transmission, and electrical equipment for determining yield;

aids in verifying test yields through exchanging geological data, (1) establishing correlation between stated yields and seismic signals; and (2) improving assessments of yields based on seismic instrument measurements;

helps reestablish momentum of arms control;

confirms that the United States is an international negotiator in good faith.

Arguments against the treaty are that it

legitimizes peaceful nuclear explosions;

continues discriminatory aspects of 1963 Limited Test Ban Treaty permitting testing only by nuclear weapon states;

undermines efforts to persuade near-nuclear countries to forgo nuclear option;

links military and peaceful uses thus lessening likelihood of reducing 150-kiloton ceiling so long as the USSR professes interest in PNEs.

weakens political support for a comprehensive test ban.

Treaties are bilateral, not multilateral.

Inspection provisions not exercised.

Status:

Executive: under review.

Legislative: hearings were held before Senate foreign relations committee in 1977; presently in committee.

With a CTB treaty in place, parties would be inhibited from deploying untested weapons, an inhibition that would reduce first-strike fears and further undercut arguments for counterforce weapons and policies. Moreover, CTB would strengthen and complement other arms control agreements, eliminate environmental and health hazards associated with the testing of nuclear weapons, and reduce the enormously debilitating diversion of wealth that is an integral feature of current nuclear strategy.[5]

No-First-Use Pledge

Speaking for the USSR before the UN Second Special Session on Disarmament in June 1982, Foreign Minister Andrei Gromyko pledged that Russia "would not be the first to use nuclear weapons."[6] The United States must now also take immediate steps to renounce the first use of nuclear weapons. Until now the U.S. interest in retaining a first-use option has been based upon fears of American conventional force inferiority in vital theaters of possible engagement. In the words of former Secretary of Defense Harold Brown:

> It continues to be U.S. policy that we will resist attacks on the United States and its allies by whatever means necessary, including nuclear weapons. We have made no secret of our view that conventional forces are an essential component of the collective deterrent and that any conventional aggression should be met initially by conventional means. We also recognize that nuclear decisions—and especially collective nuclear decisions—would be difficult and could be time-consuming, which makes strong non-nuclear

> capabilities all the more important. But the United States remains determined to do whatever is required to prevent the defeat of its own and allied forces. Our strategic and theater nuclear forces serve as the ultimate backup to our NATO commitments. Not only do they provide the means to strike NATO-related targets; they also dramatize to a potential attacker that any conventional attack could set off a chain of nuclear escalation, the consequences of which would be incalculable.[7]

But why, we might ask, should the American policy of first use appear threatening to the Soviets? After all, it has always been the official policy of the United States not to launch a nuclear strike as an initial, offensive move of war. Is there anything provocative about a nuclear strategy that does not exclude the *retaliatory* use of nuclear weapons to stave off defeat in conventional conflict?

The answer to this question lies in the fact that, in practice, the distinctions between the first use of nuclear weapons and a nuclear first strike are apt to prove meaningless. Once an American adversary had committed an act of aggression, the United States would certainly characterize any intended nuclear response as a first use rather than as a first strike. Since the determination that an act of aggression had taken place would necessarily be made by the United States rather than by some specially constituted central arbiter, it follows that certain acts that are judged to be aggressive by the United States might warrant an American nuclear response.

George F. Kennan has pointed out that this country's insistence on the option of nuclear first use has long prevented us from arriving at viable nuclear arms reduction. Since first use makes no sense if the opponent can respond in kind and since that option has rendered nuclear policy ineffective, Kennan urges its abandonment.[8]

Taken together with the consequences of NATO's conventional force inferiority, the American policy of first use is especially unsettling to the USSR since it is a policy that (1) allows for rapid escalation to nuclear conflict, (2) allows for the possibility of disguising a first strike as a first use either by deliberately creating conditions that lead to acts of aggression or by falsely alleging that such acts have actually taken place, and (3) joins with a targeting doctrine that focuses on Soviet strategic forces.

Hence the American policy of first use offers incentives to the USSR to undertake a preemptive nuclear strike against the United States. Moreover, this policy creates incentives for *other* nuclear powers to adopt hair trigger strategies for protection against possible preemptive strikes. And these risks are incurred by the United States with no real benefit in terms of deterrence, since any American nuclear retaliation (including enhanced radiation weapons) would almost certainly draw a Soviet nuclear response. In view of the enormously high probability of Soviet nuclear counterretaliation and the terrible destruction that would be visited upon allies "in order to save them," Soviet strategists must entertain grave doubts about American willingness to use theater nuclear forces. Indeed in the aftermath of an overwhelming Soviet conventional assault against American allies, it could conceivably be more rational for this country's national command authority to bypass theater nuclear forces altogether, urging instead the immediate resort to a strategic strike.

With these facts in mind, it should be clear that the United States would stand to gain from a firm renunciation of the first-use option. To allow for such a renunciation, the United States must abandon production of the neutron bomb,[9] discontinue NATO plans for the modernization of intermediate-range nuclear weapons in Western Europe, redeploy theater nuclear forces away from frontiers, and ultimately remove these forces altogether. These steps, of course, must be accompanied by significant efforts to strengthen American and allied conventional forces vis-à-vis Warsaw Pact forces in order to preserve a sufficiently high nuclear threshold.[10]

For its part, the Soviet Union should parallel American nuclear concessions by accepting far-reaching curbs on its growing capability to deliver theater nuclear weapons. Warsaw Pact forces are currently equipped with tactical nuclear delivery systems, and Moscow has deployed in the Soviet Union itself even longer range systems with a theater attack capability. These peripheral attack systems include light and medium bombers, the large MRBM (medium-range ballistic missile) and IRBM (intermediate-range ballistic missile) force being modernized with mobile SS-20 MIRVed missiles, and submarine and surface ships armed with ballistic and cruise missiles. In pursuit of an overall plan to achieve the equalization of conventional forces in the European theater (a NATO condition for meeting no-first-use agreement conditions) the USSR should also agree to substantial reductions of Warsaw Pact ground manpower and tank forces.

Presently of course negotiations are underway in Geneva and in Vienna concerning control of intermediate-range European nuclear forces and mutual balanced conventional forces on the continent. The Geneva talks flow from President Reagan's November 18, 1981, offer to cancel deployments of the Pershing II and ground-launched cruise missile (GLCM) if the Soviet Union would eliminate its SS-20, SS-4, and SS-5 missiles. The Vienna talks between NATO and the Warsaw Pact on mutual balanced force reduction (MBFR) have been going on since 1973 and are concerned with the reduction and limitation of conventional forces in Central Europe and with associated confidence-building and verification measures.

These two efforts are tied closely together, with the progress of theater nuclear reductions much dependent on what is accomplished on MBFR. This is the case because NATO's commitment to nuclear defense stems from fear of the Warsaw Pact's numerically superior conventional forces. It follows that a great deal is at stake in Vienna and that Soviet reaction to President Reagan's June 10, 1982, initiative will be watched closely in the West. This initiative, announced in Bonn, seeks common collective ceilings in the reductions area (the Federal Republic of Germany, Belgium, the Netherlands and Luxembourg in the West, and East Germany, Poland and Czechoslovakia in the East) of about 700,000 ground forces and about 900,000 ground and air forces. The NATO initiative also includes measures to encourage cooperation and verify compliance.

Should there be substantial success in producing equalization of conventional forces (a process that would require cuts in ground forces in Central Europe of about 260,000 by the Warsaw Pact and about 90,000 by NATO to achieve the proposed common ceilings), the U.S./NATO side could be expected to diminish its long-standing commitment to theater nuclear forces and to the associated policy of first use. Special consideration should be given to the key proposal offered recently by the Independent Commission on Disarmament and Security Issues, the elimination of tactical nuclear weapons from Central Europe by the end of 1983. Calling for rapid progress in U.S.–Soviet negotiations on intermediate-range nuclear weapons that threaten Europe (together with the achievement of parity, at lower levels, of conventional forces in Europe), the commission argued for substantial reductions in the nuclear stockpile leading to denuclearization in Europe. To give its recommendation greater specificity, the commission proposed the establishment of a battlefield-nuclear weapon free zone, starting with Central Europe and extending ultimately from the northern to the southern flanks of the two alliance systems. Implemented within the context of an agreement on parity and mutual force reductions in Central Europe, this scheme would prohibit nuclear munitions, storage sites for nuclear munitions, and maneuvers simulating nuclear operations inside the zone.

As the commission pointed out, the key to reducing the nuclear threat in Europe lies in the antecedent realization of approximate parity in conventional forces between the two alliances. There would be little purpose, however, in being overly preoccupied with the idea of balance in European nuclear forces as an interim objective toward total denuclearization. Such an idea would have nothing to do with the probability of nuclear weapons use by either side.

The Western arms control negotiating stance must refrain from exaggerating the interlock between Soviet and NATO theater nuclear forces. According to a recent study by George H. Quester on these issues:

> The United States and its NATO allies should generally avoid getting pulled into a comparison of totals of LRTNF systems with a view to some kind of parity . . . the negotiating formulas offered by the West should address *ratios of reductions* on the two sides, starting from the status quo at any particular moment.[11]

The control of Soviet theater nuclear forces must also not be considered apart from the theater attack capabilities of Soviet strategic forces. From the point of view of European security, there can be no meaningful control of Soviet intermediate-range nuclear weapons that leaves Soviet strategic nuclear weapons unaffected. This is the case because the longer range weapons with slight adjustments in trajectory could hit targets anywhere in Europe. Moreover the Soviet intermediate-range SS-20 missiles located on the non-European side of the Urals could destroy targets in Western Europe as easily as those that are deployed on the western side of the Urals. Even the SS-20s facing China could be moved to sites from which they could destroy NATO targets. It follows that there can be no final success in limiting intermediate-range nuclear weapons until the search for such limitation is fully joined to efforts for strategic weapons control.

There is another reason why the two arms control efforts now underway in Geneva are intimately connected. From the point of view of Soviet security, there would be little reason to agree on control of intermediate-range weapons without a coincident sense of the strategic missiles that can be brought within Soviet range. For the Soviets the largely conceptual distinctions between intermediate and strategic nuclear weapons are substantially less important than the common capacity of these weapons to strike within Soviet territory.

Although American initiatives toward no-first-use appear risky, they are considerably less dangerous than continuing on the present course. Current United States strategic policy heightens the chances for nuclear war without providing credible deterrence against Soviet conventional attack. The supposedly tough-minded argument that increased Soviet adventurism and offensive strategic policy need to be countered by a parallel American response is devoid of logical consistency. Understood in terms of careful cost/benefit calculations instead of the inflamed rhetoric of political oratory, American self-interest points unambiguously to paralleling the Soviet no-first-use pledge and to enhancing the credibility of mutual renunciation of first-use by steady progress toward conventional military parity at reduced levels. Taken together with serious movement on START, such progress would point to the beginnings of successful denuclearization in Europe.

Once commitment to a no-first-use policy has been made by the United States, steps should be taken to extend the principles of this doctrine to nonnuclear weapons states. Appropriate assurances could take the form of positive guarantees (assistance among allies in the case of nuclear threat or blackmail) or negative guarantees (pledges that the nuclear-weapon holders will not use or threaten to use nuclear weapons against states without them). At this time the United States has refused to go beyond resolution 255 of the UN Security Council (1968) in extending positive guarantees. And while there has been general support for the idea of negative security assurances, the existing pledges have been made with several critical conditions.

In 1976 the UN General Assembly invited the nuclear weapon holding states to extend assurances to states without nuclear weapons "which are not parties to the nuclear security arrangements of the nuclear powers." At the tenth special session of the General Assembly, the nuclear powers offered unilateral declarations on this question.[12] With only one exception these declarations were both conditional and limited:

United States

> The United States will not use nuclear weapons against any non–nuclear State party to the non-proliferation Treaty or to any comparable internationally binding commitment not to acquire nuclear explosive devices, except in the case of an attack on the United States, its territories or armed forces, or its allies, by such a State allied to a nuclear-weapon State or associated with a nuclear-weapon State in carrying out or sustaining the attack.

USSR

> The Soviet Union declared that it will never use nuclear weapons against those States which renounce the production and acquisition of nuclear weapons and have no nuclear weapons on their territories. We are ready to conclude special agreements to that effect with any such non-nuclear State. We call upon all other nuclear Powers to follow our example and assure similar obligations.

United Kingdom

> I accordingly give the following assurance, on behalf of my Government, to non-nuclear weapon States which are parties to the non-proliferation Treaty or to other internationally binding commitments not to manufacture or acquire nuclear explosive devices: Britain undertakes not to use nuclear weapons against such States except in the case of an attack on the United Kingdom, its dependent territories, its armed forces or its allies by such a State in association or alliance with a nuclear-weapon State.

France

> In terms of their security, the decision by the States of a region to preserve a nuclear-free status should entail an obligation for the nuclear-weapon States to refrain from seeking a military advantage from this situation. Nuclear-weapon States should in particular preclude, according to a formula to be defined, any use or threat of use of nuclear weapons against States that are part of a nuclear-free zone.

China

> We have . . . on many occasions stated that we will at no time and in no circumstances be the first to use nuclear weapons . . . A measure of urgency is for all nuclear countries to undertake not to resort to the threat or use of nuclear weapons against the non-nuclear countries and nuclear-free zones.

Unfortunately, extending the principles of a no-first-use agreement to nonnuclear weapons states would have relatively limited credibility, since there would be no concrete set of denuclearization policies to support a commitment by nuclear-weapons states not to use nuclear weapons against non-nuclear-weapons states. Moreover, a no-first-use pledge to nonnuclear weapons states would do nothing to allay the fears of these states concerning the nuclear intentions of nonnuclear adversary states. Therefore in the absence of assurances that its own compliance with nonproliferation norms would be paralleled by the compliance of nonnuclear adversary states, each nonnuclear weapons state may calculate that the benefits of "going nuclear" would outweigh the costs.

The central problem of extending the protection of no-first-use to non–nuclear-weapons states is not the absence of pertinent declarations or pledges but the uncertainty of every such state about the intentions of some other states. Although little can be done to relieve this uncertainty as far as it refers to the nuclear-weapons states, some steps can be taken concerning states without nuclear weapons, starting with a cooperative effort by the current nuclear-weapons states and nuclear-supplier states toward the goal of nonproliferation.

To be effective this effort must be directed at controlling a large number of independent national wills. Such control is an example of the general problem of decision that arises when the benefits of common action are contingent upon the expectation that certain other parties will cooperate. Understood in such terms, nonproliferation efforts will remain in doubt as long as they depend upon voluntary compliance by states that expect reciprocal compliance by certain other states. To remove this uncertainty, the current nuclear-weapons and nuclear-supplier states must move deliberately and cooperatively to control the spread of nuclear weapons and sensitive nuclear technologies.

Joint Nuclear Freeze

The United States and the USSR must implement a freeze on nuclear arms. Specifically, in the words of the freeze campaign's "Call to Halt the Nuclear Arms Race," the superpowers "should adopt a mutual freeze on the testing, production and deployment of nuclear weapons and of missiles and new aircraft designed primarily to deliver nuclear weapons." Verifiable by highly reliable national technical means, this freeze should be followed by negotiations to codify the moratorium into a formal treaty. Procedurally these negotiations might follow the precedent of the 1958–1961 nuclear weapons test moratorium, during which time testing was suspended while the United States, the USSR, and Great Britain negotiated a partial test ban treaty.

At this time the nationwide grass-roots nuclear arms freeze campaign launched at Georgetown University in spring 1981 has gained widespread support from a broad spectrum of groups and individuals. By helping to stabilize the present condition of rough parity and mutual deterrence, the freeze would impose deescalatory restraints on the current expansion of counterforce measures by both sides. And such restraints would create the conditions needed to strengthen the prospects for ultimate reductions of nuclear weapons and for a more reliable nonproliferation regime. Consider the following excerpt from the text of the freeze proposal now gaining widespread support in the United States:

> To improve national and international security, the United States and the Soviet Union should stop the nuclear arms race. Specifically, they should adopt a mutual freeze on the testing, production and deployment of nuclear weapons and of missiles and new aircraft designed primarily to deliver nuclear weapons. This is an essential, verifiable first step toward lessening the risk of nuclear war and reducing the nuclear arsenals.
>
> The horror of a nuclear holocaust is universally acknowledged. Today, the United States and the USSR possess 50,000 nuclear weapons. In a half hour a fraction of these weapons can destroy all cities in the northern hemisphere. Yet over the next decade, the two countries, between them, plan to build over 20,000 more nuclear warheads, along with a new generation of nuclear missiles and aircraft.
>
> The weapon programs of the next decade, if not stopped, will pull the nuclear tripwire tighter. Counterforce and other nuclear war-fighting systems will improve the ability of the United States and the USSR to attack the opponent's nuclear forces and other military targets. This will increase the pressure on both sides to use their nuclear weapons in a crisis rather than risk losing them in a first strike.
>
> Such developments will increase hair-trigger readiness for a massive nuclear exchange at a time when economic difficulties, political dissension, revolution, and competition for energy supplies may be rising worldwide. At the same time more countries may acquire nuclear weapons. Unless we change this combination of trends, the danger of nuclear war will be greater in the late 1980s and 1990s than ever before.
>
> Rather than permit this dangerous future to evolve, the United States and the Soviet Union should stop the nuclear arms race.
>
> A freeze on nuclear missiles and aircraft can be verified by existing national means. A total freeze can be verified more easily than the complex SALT I

and II agreements. The freeze on warhead production could be verified by the safeguards of the International Atomic Energy Agency. Stopping the production of nuclear weapons and weapon-grade material and applying the safeguards to U.S. and Soviet nuclear programs would increase the incentive of other countries to adhere to the nonproliferation treaty, renouncing acquisition of their own nuclear weapons, and to accept the same safeguards.

A freeze would hold constant the existing nuclear parity between the United States and the Soviet Union. By precluding production of counterforce weaponry on either side, it would eliminate excuses for further arming on both sides. Later, following the immediate adoption of the freeze, its terms should be negotiated into the more durable form of a treaty.

A nuclear-weapon freeze accompanied by government-aided conversion of nuclear industries would save at least $100 billion each in U.S. and Soviet military spending (at today's prices) in 1981–1990. This would reduce inflation. The savings could be applied to balance the budget, reduce taxes, improve services, subsidize renewable energy, or increase aid to poverty-stricken Third World regions. By shifting personnel to more labor-intensive civilian jobs, a nuclear-weapon freeze would also raise employment.

Stopping the U.S.–Soviet nuclear arms race is the single most useful step that can be taken now to reduce the likelihood of nuclear war and to prevent the spread of nuclear weapons to more countries. This step is a necessary prelude to creating international conditions in which:

Further steps can be taken toward a stable, peaceful international order.

The threat of first use of nuclear weaponry can be ended.

The freeze can be extended to other nations.

The nuclear arsenals on all sides can be drastically reduced or eliminated, making the world truly safe from the possibility of nuclear destruction.

Statement on the Nuclear-Weapon Freeze Proposal

Scope of the Freeze

1. Underground nuclear tests should be suspended, pending final agreement on a comprehensive test ban treaty.
2. There should be a freeze on testing, production, and deployment of all missiles and new aircraft that have nuclear weapons as their sole or main payload. This includes:

U.S. Delivery Vehicles	*Soviet Delivery Vehicles*
In production	In production
Improved Minuteman ICBM	SS-19 ICBM
Trident I SLBM	SS-N-18 SLBM
Air-launched cruise missile (ALCM)	SS-20 IRBM
	Backfire bomber
In development	In development
MX ICBM	SS-17, SS-18, SS-19 ICBM improvements
Trident II SLBM	

Long-range ground- and sea-launched cruise missiles (GLCM, SLCM)	New ICBM
Pershing II IRBM	New SLBM (SS-N-20)
New bomber	

3. The number of land- and submarine-based launch tubes for nuclear missiles should be frozen. Replacement submarines could be built to keep the force constant but with no net increase in SLBM tubes and no new missiles.
4. No further MIRVing or other changes to existing missiles or bomber loads would be permitted.

All of the above measures can be verified by existing national means of verification with high confidence.

The following measures cannot be verified nationally with the same confidence, but an effort should be made to include them:

5. Production of fissionable material (enriched uranium and plutonium) for weapon purposes should be halted.
6. Production of nuclear weapons (bombs) should be halted.

There are two arguments for attempting to include these somewhat less verifiable steps. First, with a halt to additional and new delivery vehicles, there will be no need for additional bombs. Thus production of weapon-grade fissionable material and bombs would probably stop in any event. Second, the establishment of a *universal* ban on production of weapon-grade fissionable material and nuclear bombs, verified by international inspection as established now for non–nuclear-weapon states under the nonproliferation treaty and the International Atomic Energy Agency, would greatly strengthen that treaty and improve the prospects for halting the spread of nuclear weapons.

Relation to START Negotiations

The bilateral freeze is aimed at being introduced as soon as sufficient popular and political support is developed to move the governments toward its adoption. The freeze would prevent dangerous developments in the absence of a START treaty. It would preclude exploitation of loopholes in past treaties and, at the same time, satisfy critics who are concerned that the START process may not succeed in stopping the arms race. The freeze does not replace the START negotiating process, but should supplement and strengthen it.

Economic Benefits.

Although nuclear forces take only a small part of U.S. and Soviet military spending, they do cost some tens of billions of dollars annually. About half of these funds go to existing nuclear forces, while half are budgeted for the testing, production, and deployment of new warheads and delivery systems. A nuclear-weapon freeze, accompanied by government-aided conversion of nuclear industries to civilian production, would yield several important economic benefits:

About $100 billion each (at 1981 prices) would be saved by the United States and the Soviet Union over the period from 1981 to 1990 in unnecessary military spending.

The savings could be applied to balance the budget; reduce taxes; improve services now being cut back; subsidize home and commercial conversion to safe, renewable energy resources; or increase economic aid to poverty-stricken Third World regions, thereby defusing some of the time bombs of international conflict.

With the shift of personnel to more labor-intensive civilian jobs, employment would rise. At the same time, the highly inflationary pressure of military spending would be mitigated.

Verification

The comprehensive nature of a total freeze on nuclear weapon testing, production, and deployment (and, by implication, development) would facilitate verification. Long-range bomber and missile production would be proscribed. The letter of assurance attached to the draft SALT II treaty that the USSR will not increase its rate of production of Backfire bombers indicates not only *deployment* but also *production* of the relatively large aircraft and missiles in question can be observed with considerable confidence. Although concealed production and stockpiling of aircraft and missiles is theoretically possible, it would be extraordinarily difficult to accomplish with no telltale construction or supply. Any attempt would require the building or modification of plants and the development of new transport lines that are not operational at present. It would also involve high risks of detection and high penalties in worsening relations without offering any significant strategic advantage.

Verification of a ban on *tests* of missiles designed to carry nuclear weapons can be provided with high confidence by existing satellite and other detection systems. Here, too, a comprehensive approach is easier to verify than a partial or limited one.

Verification of aircraft, missile, and submarine deployments, by specific quantity, is already provided under the terms of the SALT II and SALT I treaty language. Verifying *no* additional deployments or major modifications will be considerably easier in fact than checking compliance with specific numerical ceilings in a continually changing environment. Verification of a comprehensive nuclear weapon test ban, the subject of study and negotiation for many years, has been determined to be possible within the terms of the existing draft comprehensive test ban treaty.

Initiatives Toward the Freeze

Either the United States or the USSR could initiate movement toward the freeze by taking modest, unilateral steps that would demonstrate its good faith, start movement in the right direction, and make it easier for the other country to take a similar step. For example, either country could

1. undertake a three-month moratorium on nuclear test explosions, to be extended if reciprocated;
2. stop further deployment, for a specified period, of one new strategic weapon or improvement of an existing weapon;
3. draw up and publish comprehensive conversion plans for the nuclear facilities and employment that would be affected by a freeze, as a sign of serious commitment to the goal.

Nuclear-Weapon-Free Zones

The superpowers must also take further steps toward wider arrangements for nuclear-weapon-free zones. The concept of such zones has already received international legal expression in the Treaty for the Prohibition of Nuclear Weapons in Latin America (the Treaty of Tlatelolco), which entered into force on April 22, 1968, and the two additional protocols to the treaty. Unlike two earlier treaties that seek to limit the spread of nuclear weapons into areas yet to be contaminated—the Antarctic treaty of 1961 and the Outer Space Treaty of 1967—the Latin American treaty concerns a populated area. The terms of the treaty include measures to prevent the type of deployment of nuclear weapons that led to the Cuban missile crisis, methods of verification by both the parties themselves and by their own regional organization, and International Atomic Energy Agency safeguards on all nuclear materials and facilities under the jurisdiction of the parties.

The potential value of nuclear weapon free zones has been underscored several times by the United Nations. In its resolution of December 11, 1975 (3472 B: XXX), the General Assembly stated that "nuclear weapon free zones constitute one of the most effective means for preventing the proliferation, both horizontal and vertical, of nuclear weapons and for contributing to the elimination of the danger of nuclear holocaust." Subsequently, on June 30, 1978, the General Assembly, in the program of action adopted by consensus at its special session devoted to disarmament, proclaimed that "the process of establishing such zones in different parts of the world should be encouraged with the ultimate objective of achieving a world entirely free of nuclear weapons.[13]

In June 1981 the USSR showed a promising interest in enlarging the scope of the nuclear-weapons-free zone idea. President Brezhnev offered Nordic nations a guarantee against Soviet nuclear attack in exchange for their creation of a Northern European nuclear-free zone. This idea, which was first advanced twenty years ago by Finland, which borders the Soviet Kola Peninsula, could be accomplished either by concluding a multilateral agreement or by bilateral agreements with each of the states participating in the zone. According to Brezhnev, since nuclear weapons have not yet been deployed in northern Europe, a nuclear-weapons-free zone in the region could "seal and legally formalize" the area's nonnuclear status.

An initiative on nuclear-weapon-free zones has been taken by the United States in August 1981. Eugene V. Rostow, director of the U.S. Arms Control and Disarmament Agency, announced that this country has begun to seek an accord to keep the Middle East free of nuclear weapons. Although he insisted that no specific plan has yet been formulated, the idea will be to pattern it after the Treaty of Tlatelolco. According to Rostow:

> We have no plan yet, no draft of a treaty, except that the Treaty of Tlatelolco will be a rough model in everybody's mind as they move forward on this venture. And I think it has very high potential. It is a natural response to the risks of proliferation which have become much worse in recent years.[14]

The risks and consequences of nuclear proliferation in the Middle East are especially apparent in the aftermath of Israel's raid on Iraq's nuclear reactor on June 7, 1981, and the resultant call, by Iraq's President Saddam Hussein for Arab nuclear weapons (sixteen days later). Rather than remove the problem, the destruction of the Osirak reactor seems to have accelerated Arab preparations to "go nuclear." Iraq will almost certainly try to rebuild its reactor in a fashion that would preclude another successful attack and Egypt has already undertaken an ambitious nuclear program.

In view of former Israeli Chief of Staff Motta Gur's contention that "the next Arab-Israeli war, if it occurs, will bring us to the edge of a nuclear confrontation,"[15] it is vital that appropriate steps toward denuclearization of the region be taken immediately. Serious consideration must be given to Israeli Prime Minister Begin's proposal on June 18, 1982, before the U.N. General Assembly's Second Special Session on Disarmament, for a Middle East nuclear-weapons-free zone. And to make such consideration possible, there must first be substantial progress toward comprehensive resolution of the Israeli–Arab conflict, one wherein "rejectionist" Arab states agree to recognize Israel's right to exist and where all parties create a proper solution to the Palestinian problem.

Taken together with other nonproliferation efforts, especially the nonproliferation treaty, the international nuclear fuel cycle evaluation (INFCE), and the safeguard activities of the International Atomic Energy Agency, nuclear-weapon-free zones warrant especially serious attention by the superpowers. Although Soviet support for these zones in certain regions seems aimed largely at reducing the American nuclear presence, it is by no means clear that such reductions would give military or political advantage to the USSR. Indeed in view of what has already been said about the dangers and unreliability of theater nuclear deterrence, the overall security effect of such American reductions would certainly be gainful for the United States.

By limiting the importance of nuclear weapons through support for CTB, no-first-use pledges, and nuclear-weapon-free zones, the superpowers could offer the non–nuclear-weapons states a significant incentive not to proliferate. However, additional steps are needed to curtail the transfer of certain commercial nuclear facilities and materials. Since access to a nuclear weapons capability now depends largely on the policies of a small group of supplier states, such policies constitute a vital element of nonproliferation efforts. In the years ahead states that carry on international trade in nuclear facilities, technology, and materials will have to improve and coordinate their export policies.

A major part of the problem, of course, is the fact that nuclear exports, while they contribute to the spread of nuclear weapons, are a lucrative market for a supplier state. Moreover in certain exchanges such exports are also a crucial political lever in assuring access to oil. Recognizing the conflict in objectives between nonproliferation and a nuclear export market, the International Atomic Energy Agency, Euratom, and the Treaty on the Nonproliferation of Nuclear Weapons impose obligations on nuclear exports concerning the development of nuclear explosives. Article 1 of the treaty pledges the signatories "not in any way to assist, encourage, or induce any non-nuclear weapon State to manufacture or otherwise acquire nuclear weapons or other nuclear explosive devices." At the same time, article 4 ensures that "All parties to the Treaty undertake to facilitate, and have the right to participate in, the fullest possible exchange of equipment, materials, and scientific and technological information for the peaceful uses of nuclear energy." In this connection unilateral American conditions on this country's nuclear material exports are imposed by the Nuclear Nonproliferation Act of 1978 (NNPA).

As long as the world system fails to provide vulnerable states with a reasonable assurance of protection against nuclear attack, such states will feel compelled to continue to rely on the remedy of self-help. Understood in terms of past and future preemptive air strikes against nuclear reactors or nuclear weapons, this suggests that the principal enemies of nonproliferation are states that have undertaken imprudent sales of nuclear technologies and materials to unstable countries. The United States must bear a certain responsibility for nonproliferation failures because it has failed to dissuade its allies from their shortsighted excursions in nuclear commerce.

The time has come for states to struggle with the painful movements of the lungfish, forcing old fins to become new legs. For those that lock their definitions of national interest into the dying forms of *realpolitik*, there can be only disaster. Faced with the awareness that the wavelength of change is now shorter than the life span of man, states must replace the intransigence of nationalisms with faith in a new kind of power. This is the primordial power of unity and interdependence, an ecumenical power that can replace the centrifugal forces that have atomized nations with a fresh vision of realism.

To accomplish the objectives of nonproliferation, it is not enough to provide the customary restraints offered by international treaties and institutions. Although such restraints are essential, they must be surrounded by a new field of consciousness, one flowing from a common concern for the human species and from the undimmed communion of individual states with the entire system of states. Living at an interface between world order and global disintegration, states must break the shackles of outmoded forms of self-interest. With the explosion of the myth of realism, the global society of states could begin to come together in a renewed understanding of the connection between survival and relatedness. When this happens, states will finally consummate their search for planetization.

Our task, then, is to make the separate states conscious of their emerging planetary identity. With such a revisioning of national goals and incentives, states can progress from the vapid clichés of realism to an awareness of new archetypes for global society. Since all things contain their own contradiction, the world system based upon militaristic nationalism can be transformed into an organic world society.

To succeed in this task will be very difficult. But it need not be as fanciful as some would have us believe. Indeed, before we take the shroud measurements of the corpse of human society, we must understand that faith in the new forms of international interaction is a critical step toward their implementation. Or as we learn from Albert Camus's *Neither Victims nor Executioners*, "History is simply man's desperate effort to give body to his most clairvoyant dreams."

We are, as philosopher William Irwin Thompson suggests, at the "edge of history." It is a time to transcend the clogged conduits of national military power and to reaffirm that the truest forms of realism lie in the imaginings of idealists. In the words of Thompson:

> In the history of ideas a new idea is often first picked up by a crazy person, then elaborated by an artist who is more interested in its imaginative possibilities than in its literal truth; then it is picked up by a scholar or scientist who has become familiar with the idea through the work of the artist; the savant makes the hitherto crazy idea perfectly acceptable to the multitude, until finally the idea rests as a certainty in the hands of a bureaucracy of pedants.[16]

Thompson's use of the term "crazy person" is, of course, laced with irony. In a world wherein "sane" foreign policy is still tied to the preposterous lies of a "peace through arms race" ideology, sanity can lead only to oblivion. In such a world, only a crazy person can harbor the kind of consciousness that is needed for survival. Time, as St. Augustine wrote, is more than the present as we experience it and the past as a present memory. It is also the future as a present expectation, and this expectation carries within itself the seeds of its own verification.

To fulfill the expectations of a new global society, one based on a more advanced stage of world evolutionary development, appropriate initiatives must be taken *within* states. Here is the primary arena of world order reform. Yet, national leaders can never be expected to initiate the essential changes on their own. Rather, the new evolutionary vanguard must grow out of informed publics throughout the world.

Once established, such a vanguard must seek to end the competitiveness of states that is founded upon egotistic definitions of national interest. The replacement of the power of the individual state by the power of the entire global community constitutes the decisive step of planetization. This power of the entire global community must not be the coercive military power encountered in recommendations for world government but the power of a universalized and new consciousness, a clear vision of reality that substitutes wholeness and convergence for the fatal instincts of narcissism.

But why not world government? Through the centuries, the idea has persisted that decentralized global politics cannot provide world order reform, and that true security requires nothing less than the replacement of balance-of-power dynamics with world government. In a world system teeming with the implements of apocalyptic destruction, is this idea not particularly valid?

While the questions surrounding world government are enormously complex, there is really no reason to believe that fundamental transformations of the existing pattern of military force and sovereign authority are an appropriate path to avoidance of nuclear war. The establishment of world government would continue reliance on the logic of deterrence. With the creation of world government, nothing would be done to change the threat system dynamics of the prevailing balance of power. True, threats would now be issued "from above" rather than laterally, but nothing would be done to eliminate the underlying notion of security through fear.

With today's enormously destructive weapons technologies, it is imperative that the shortcomings of world federal government be widely understood. National decision makers must learn to appreciate that the allegedly realistic approach to security is actually unrealistic (an approach that ties security to relative power position) and that long-term security via nuclear deterrence is a contradiction in terms. This is true whether threats of retaliatory destruction originate horizontally from other states in the classical balance-of-power arrangement or vertically from the specially constituted world public authority.

But what of those conceptions of world federal government that envision disarmed states and a lightly armed world government force? Clark and Sohn call for "universal and complete national disarmament together with the establishment of institutions corresponding in the world field to those which maintain law and order within local communities and nations.[17] And the World Federalists, USA, consistently call for a schedule for universal and complete disarmament rather than for a system whereby order is maintained by the perpetual threat of retaliatory destruction from above.

Even these conceptions are not immune to the foregoing critique of world federal government, however. How is such a program for disarmament to be accomplished, after all? Is it to be without a prior transfer of strategic and conventional military force to the specially constituted world government center? If so, what reasons exist to believe that individual states will calculate that the benefits of disarmament will exceed the costs if all of the other states are willing to disarm and that all of the other states are willing to disarm?

Clearly, unless the specially constituted world government operates on the basis of threat-system dynamics that are supported by the capability to yield assured destruction, each state contemplating disarmament will entertain grave doubts about the reciprocal behavior of all of the other states. Since the prospect of disarmament can be considered gainful by each state only if it is expected to be generally paralleled, these doubts have fatal implications for the success of disarmament. Without a prior transfer of military force to the world federal government, individual states contemplating disarmament would have every reason to calculate that the prospective costs of compliance with the decision to disarm would outweigh the prospective benefits.

What all of this means is that even conceptions of world federal government that rest upon designs for disarmament must take into account the foregoing criticisms. This is because disarmament simply cannot be wished into being but must be accomplished incrementally.

The primary stages of disarmament necessarily require conditions whereby the world government center is in a position to influence effectively the decisionmaking of states such that the prospective costs of failing to disarm appear intolerably high. And this necessarily requires a continuation (however temporary) of the long-standing threat system dynamics of deterrence. A world government that fulfills the requirements of a credible deterrence posture in the nuclear age is an essential precursor to a world government superintending a disarmed world with light police-type forces. Hence, the weaknesses of the former conception cannot be overlooked by those who favor the second.

From the standpoint of feasibility or attainability, moreover, it is exceedingly doubtful that even the primary variant of world federal government stands much hope of creation. Centralization might be achieved coercively as well as volitionally, of course, and Caesarism as a path to world peace through world government need not be dismissed out of hand. At the same time as Rousseau recognized long ago, it is a path that is likely to occasion the very sorts of conflicts and calamities that it is designed to prevent.

This is not to suggest by any means, that we abandon disarmament as a vital objective of world order reform. While world government is not a promising path to world order reform and while it would not provide an appropriate means of nuclear weapons reduction, disarmament can and should be pursued within the improved context of decentralized world politics. Such improvement could be brought about by a progressive transformation of conflictual foreign policies within states and by the associated development of arms control and nonproliferation strategies.

For disarmament to work, it is not enough that states prefer the conditions of a disarmed world to those of the present. Before states will calculate that the prospective benefits of disarmament exceed the prospective costs, they will have to believe that their own willingness to disarm will be generally enough reciprocated by certain other states. In the absence of such a belief, they will calculate that disarmament is more costly than gainful.

Disarmament therefore is a particular instance of the general problem of ensuring an adequate supply of collective goods. As long as each state lacks assurances about the reciprocal behavior of other states, it is apt to calculate that security can be more gainfully maximized privately than cooperatively. For each state to calculate otherwise, it would need strong assurances that a sufficient number of other states will abide by the cooperative search for security.

The problem is illustrated nicely by Rousseau's parable of the stag hunt in *A Discourse on the Origin of Inequality*. In this little tale five hungry men agree to cooperate in a stag hunt. But as a hare happens to cross the path of one of them during the hunt, he grabs it. In so doing, he allows the stag to escape and the would be fruits of cooperation are lost to the other hunters.

As in Rousseau's parable, states are always tempted to grab for the hare of expanded relative military power position in the search for security. Hence the more satisfactory condition of disarmament,the stag, is allowed to get away. And it is permitted to get away even though every state might agree that security would be obtained more satisfactorily in a disarmed world than in the present competitive one.

To change these conditions such that states will come to expect far-reaching compliance with disarmament obligations, all of the aforementioned improvements in world politics must first be realized. Disarmament cannot be seriously pursued amid the precarious crosscurrents of international belligerence and mistrust. Rather, it must await the achievement of a more harmonious nuclear regime, one founded on the kinds of strategic revisions and arms control agreements just discussed. With the appearance of such a regime, the START process could proceed to the negotiation of actual reductions in strategic forces, and meaningful disarmament negotiations could be extended on a fully multilateral basis.

However urgent it is to get underway with what has come to be known as real reductions in strategic forces, it would be a serious error to seek these reductions prematurely. As revealed by the unsuccessful mission to Moscow by Secretary of State Cyrus Vance in 1977, an improved nuclear regime must be constructed incrementally.[18] While it would be a monumental error to abandon disarmament for less ambitious arms control remedies, it would be just as debilitating to seek disarmament before such remedies are in place. Before states can be expected to trust that disarmament measures will be generally enough respected, they will require antecedent assurances of strategic cooperation and goodwill.

It is with this understanding that we can examine the recent proposals by George F. Kennan for a 50 percent reduction in U.S. and Soviet nuclear arsenals. According to Kennan

> What I would like to see the President do after due consultation with the Congress, would be to propose to the Soviet government an immediate across-the-boards reduction by fifty percent of the nuclear arsenals now being maintained by the superpowers—a reduction affecting in equal measure all forms of the weapons, strategic, medium range, and tactical, as well as all means of their delivery—all this to be implemented at once and without further wrangling among the experts, and to be subject to such national means of verification as now lie at the disposal of the two powers.[19]

Although Kennan's proposal comes from an acute awareness of the terrible urgency of planetary danger, it offers no real hope for real security.[20] The situation is certainly as desperate as Kennan suggests, but there is no reason to believe that the superpowers can move from *realpolitik* to world order overnight. Before any of these proposals can be implemented, a full-fledged transformation of current American nuclear strategy must take place. Such transformation is the essential primary arena of nuclear war avoidance. However slow and painstaking it might be to accomplish, it cannot be bypassed.

Sadly, no evidence exists that such transformation is now underway. Although President Reagan's latest proposals for arms control call for deep cuts in Soviet and American nuclear forces, they involve no significant changes in American nuclear strategy. The May 9, 1982, speech at Eureka College was relatively free of strident rhetoric and confrontational polemics but offered no plan to curtail this country's massive and provocative nuclear weapons buildup. As we have already seen, the president's proposal seeks a reduction in the number of nuclear warheads (and subsequently in the total payload capacity of each superpower's ballistic missiles) without modifying in any way current plans for the deployment of the MX ICBM, the B-1 bomber, European-based missiles, Trident II missiles, or C^3I (command, control, communications, and intelligence) refinements.

Evidence for the continuity of these plans was offered only two days after the president's speech by both General John W. Vessey, Jr., in testimony before the Senate arms services committee, and by then Secretary of State Alexander Haig, in testimony before the Senate foreign relations committee. General Vessey's testimony, which concerned his nomination as chairman of the joint chiefs of staff, was cast in terms of coping with alleged "Soviet nuclear superiority" (ironically, since he also indicated that "not on your life" would he exchange our nuclear forces for those of the USSR) while Secretary Haig's comments tied the prospects for successful arms control to Congressional support for the administration's $180 billion nuclear "revitalization" program.

Moreover, since the president's proposal seems one-sided in favor of the United States, it is hardly likely to create the conditions for meaningful dialogue and agreement. From the Soviet point of view, a call for cuts in land-based arsenals seems especially disadvantageous because ground-based missiles are the backbone of Soviet strategic forces. Hence Soviet leaders believe that President Reagan's proposal seeks to take advantage of structural differences in nuclear arsenals in order to ensure American military superiority over the USSR. This argument is founded upon the understanding that the USSR has about 70 percent of its warheads on ground-based missiles compared with about 20 percent for the United States.

What, then, is to be done? A promising answer is offered by Robert C. Johansen:

> To move toward a more appropriate security system we must first understand that most major governments, if left to their own pursuits, will not lead the way to a better security system. Those who hold the reins of national military power do not want to relinquish them.

It follows, says Johansen, that we must begin to exploit the potential for a broad-based popular movement against the war system.

> More and more people are aware that rationality is on the side of a secure global community, not national armaments. The question is: who will pioneer the belief that social transformation is possible? Will it be you and I, or, lacking courage and conviction, will we wait for another generation to take up this challenge, perhaps after entire continents have been despoiled with radioactive fallout . . . ? Once a sufficient number of people are committed, enough pressure can be brought to bear on governing elites and their supporters to convince them that their political careers will depend on reducing the share of taxpayers' money going into war equipment. Then officials will take seriously the need to build a more just and peaceful world order in which military power will have no role.[21]

Although Johansen's proposals are especially far-reaching, going beyond nuclear war avoidance to the end of all militaristic nationalism, their call for a raised public consciousness and an associated social movement are right on the mark.[22] Before the progressive elimination of nuclear weapons can take place, citizens of our planet must begin to prevail upon their governments to retreat from the chimera of relative advantage through nuclear arms. Understood in terms of the need to reverse current American nuclear strategy, this suggests an enlarged chorus of conscious and conscientious voices urging rapid movement toward minimum deterrence, a comprehensive test ban, American renunciation of the right to first use of nuclear weapons, a U.S.–Soviet nuclear freeze, and additional nuclear-weapons-free zones.

In the United States, the antinuclear-war movement, especially the freeze campaign, is now of considerable size and influence. Even before the beginning of the U.N. Second Special Session on Disarmament, a *New York Times* and CBS news poll in spring 1982 found that 72 percent of Americans favor a nuclear freeze. And the freeze effort is only a part of a larger grass-roots movement nationwide against nuclear weapons and nuclear war, a burgeoning critical mass of people from all walks of life with an already demonstrated ability to affect presidential decisionmaking. Indeed, the size and diversity of the antinuclear movement in the United States was illustrated most dramatically by the disarmament rally held in New York City on the eve of the second special session, in which an estimated 700,000 people participated, making it the largest political demonstration in the history of the United States.

What does all of this mean? In the first place it suggests that fear of nuclear peril is now far-reaching. Such fear is a manifestly healthy development, since it provides the necessary starting point for constructive action against the nuclear arms race. In striking confirmation of the conclusions reached in the 1978 study by Yankelovich, Skelly and White, commissioned by the Institute for World Order, the growth in public understanding of the dangers of nuclear war has been paralleled by the growth in public involvement against the nuclear arms race.

In the second place it suggests that the people of the United States are able to match the anti–nuclear war sentiments of their counterparts across the Atlantic. Just as the European Nuclear Disarmament (END) campaign has initiated a transcontinental movement for the expulsion of nuclear weapons and bases from European soil and territorial waters, so can the American anti–nuclear movement affect the progress of political efforts against nuclear war in this country. In its replication and enlargement of the social movement against nuclear weapons and nuclear war in Europe, the new American peace effort can begin to reverse the lethal trajectory of current U.S. strategic policy.

As Jean Genet suggests in *The Thief's Journal*, we live in fear of metamorphoses. Yet, we must liberate ourselves from such fear lest we capitulate to unprecedented barbarism and despair. To accomplish such liberation, citizens of the United States and other countries must continue to confront their own national military megamachinery with an alternative logic of informed opposition.

The theoretical underpinnings of such an understanding are contained in a recent article by Richard A. Falk.[23] Examining normative initiatives that challenge the root assumptions of militarization, Falk links these initiatives to actual and promising social forces. In connection with this effort, primary attention is focused upon "the Third System," which is the system of power represented by people acting individually or collectively through voluntary institutions and associations, including churches and labor unions; a system oriented around challenging the domestic manifestations of militarization.[24] Viewed as "the main bearer of new values, demands, and visions," the third system must contend with the constraints of the first system ("the system of power comprised by the governing structures of territorial states") and the second system ("the system of power comprised by the United Nations and to a lesser extent by regional international institutions").[25]

Falk's third system is of course the essential primary arena for nuclear war avoidance and world order reform. Since the first system stands firmly behind the "logic" of militarization and the second system is essentially a creature of the first system, we require a third system movement for demilitarization. Based upon the emergence of a planetary consciousness "that is alive to the interlinked dimensions of militarization," this movement must be geared to changing the orientations of first system leaders by building upward pressures from the third and second Systems.[26]

Understood in terms of the overriding global imperative to delegitimize nuclear weapons, Falk's proposal seeks a normative initiative on a global scale to create all varieties of denuclearization. Citing the examples of two documents drafted and endorsed by private citizens from around the world—the 1978 Delhi Declaration for a Just World and the 1980 Lisbon Declaration on Denuclearization for a Just World, the Failure of Nonproliferation—he encourages the continuing development of a third system consensus on the menace of nuclear weaponry. To allow for such development, special responsibility lies with citizens of the superpowers, who must encourage such demilitarizing imperatives as opposition in the United States to specific weapons systems such as MX and Trident and to the struggle for human rights in the USSR.

Although some of Falk's prescriptions are potentially contradictory (a successful movement against draft registration might heighten reliance on nuclear weapons), the underlying thesis is markedly important and warrants widespread attention: It behooves every living person to reverse the arms race and create a more harmonious configuration of planetary political life.

For such a configuration to come about, this imperative must be widely felt and collectively manifested through coherent and well-articulated transnational movements. By displaying the kind of higher loyalty contained within the idea of a Nuremberg obligation to resist crimes of state, individuals across the world can endow this strategy of world-order reform with real potency.

Epilogue

In his book *Janus: A Summing Up*, Arthur Koestler identifies the polarity between self-assertive and integrative tendencies as a universal characteristic of life.[27] Order and stability can prevail only when the two tendencies are in equilibrium. If one tendency dominates the other, the result is an end to the essential delicate balance.

This balance must immediately be restored among states in world politics. To create the necessary equilibrium, states must begin to fashion their foreign policies on a new set of premises, one that defines national interest in terms of what is best for the world system as a whole. By supplanting competitive self-seeking with cooperative self-seeking and by renouncing the "every man for himself" principle in world affairs, states can begin to move away from the social Darwinism ethic that would otherwise assure our oblivion. By building upon the understanding that it is in each state's best interests to develop foreign policy from a systemic vantage point, by defining national interests in terms of strategies that secure and sustain the entire system of states, national leaders can begin to match the awesome agenda of world order reform with effective strategies of response. With such a starting point the prevention of global nuclear catastrophe could draw its animating vision from the wisdom of Pierre Teilhard de Chardin in *The Phenomenon of Man*: "The egocentric ideal of a future reserved for those who have managed to attain egoistically the extremity of 'everyone for himself' is false and against nature. No element could move and grow except with and by all the others with itself."

The false communion of nation-states is inwardly rotten, time-dishonored, close to collapsing. A communion based on fear and dread, its mighty efforts at producing increasingly destructive weapons have occasioned a deep desolation of the human spirit. The world has conquered technology only to lose its soul.

"The world, as it is now," Herman Hesse wrote, in *Demian*, "wants to die, wants to perish—and it will." No doubt, were he alive today, Hesse would see no need to change that observation. Indeed as an anticipatory vision of what lies ahead, it is more exquisitely attuned to the present moment than to its intended time. To alter this vision, to render it inaccurate, thinking, feeling human beings will have to learn to develop their potential for cohesion with others to ever more distant boundaries.

There exist much higher reaches of planetary interaction than we are currently prepared to appreciate. These reaches must begin to be sought and cultivated. Only then will an appropriate transformation of international society become possible.

We must aim at the realization of the unique and fulfilled state in harmony with all others; a coherent vision sparked by the impulse of human singularity. With the manifestation of the one in the many, each individual state may begin to pursue a progressive development of consciousness to ever higher levels without disregard for its cumulative effects. The consequences of this principle for world order could embrace the beginnings of a new world politics.

Alas, what reasons do we have to believe that such development can ever come to pass, that states can ever free themselves from self-imposed inconscience? If, as Schiller points out, "The law of the world is the history of the world," there is certainly very little cause for faith in human progress. Such faith was basically a thing of which the ancient and medieval peoples had little conception, an idea, in fact, widely disavowed before Fontenelle and Condorcet offered it to the eighteenth-century world of letters. Even during the Renaissance, the conviction was widespread that man's development after a glorious antiquity had been regressive rather than progressive. The path of late Renaissance disillusionment is clearly marked out by Luther, Montaigne, Machiavelli, and Galileo.

During the nineteenth century a thread of hope in human progress characterized such creations as the poetry of Tennyson and the writings of Herbert Spencer, a thread that was to be broken by the incomparable barbarisms of our own century. That thread has yet to be mended. We stand in a condition of near desperation, sustained not by the hope that we can do better but by the wish (however unreasonable) that perhaps somehow we can still avoid the worst. In our profound sense of impotence, we have given new meaning to Alexander Pope's comment, "Whatever is, is right."

If it is important that states learn to care for themselves and each other at the same time, then they must begin to restore the broken thread of hope. But this is only a beginning. States must learn to supplant their misconceived separation of national interest and world interest with an ongoing commitment to planetization. Unlike anything else, this commitment can endow the search for safety from nuclear war with real hopefulness.

Will it work? Can humankind be expected to grasp this calculus of potentiality, reaffirming the sovereignty of reason over the forces of disintegration? Can states be expected to tear down the walls of competitive power struggles and replace them with the permeable membranes of spirited cooperation?

Perhaps not, but there is surely no other way. So long as individual states continue to identify their own security with the acquisition of destructive weaponry they will have only war. The Talmud tells us, "The dust from which the first man was made was gathered in all the corners of the world." By moving toward a new planetary identity, the people of Earth can begin to build bridges over the most dangerous abyss they have ever known. It is hoped that in this absurd theatre of modern world politics, human beings will choose life rather than death. Stripped of false hopes and without illusion, we may yet stare at the specter of nuclear apocalypse with passionate attention and experience the planetary responsibility that will bring liberation.

Notes

1. Even if the United States were to experience certain difficulties in getting the USSR to reciprocate the proposed initiatives, there would be no deleterious effect on American security. Indeed the net effect on American security of even unreciprocated initiatives would be gainful. This is the case because current United States nuclear policy is founded upon weapons systems and strategies that actually *undermine* the system of mutual deterrence. Contrary to the conventional wisdom that suggests American initiatives must lead to unilateral disarmament, the proposed initiatives would leave this country with a still-awesome and secure potential for nuclear retaliation. After all, the United States would seize these deescalatory initiatives without diminishing its capacity for assured destruction of the USSR.

2. See "Comprehensive Test Ban," Committee for National Security, *Fact Sheet*, October 6, 1981.

3. White Paper by the Committee for National Security, *An Arms Control Agenda for the Eighties*, Washington, D.C., June 30, 1981.

4. "Threshold Test Ban Treaty," and "Treaty on Underground Nuclear Explosions for Peaceful Purposes." Committee for National Security, *Fact Sheet,* October 6, 1981.

5. *Arms Control Agenda,* pp. 13–16.

6. A recommendation for the total prohibition of the use of nuclear weapons was adopted by the UN General Assembly in 1961 and reaffirmed in 1978. Most of the nuclear powers, however, have rejected this proposal. With respect to a no-first-use proposal among the nuclear powers, only China and the USSR have made such a pledge. The USSR has also proposed that agreement be reached on the no-first-use of both nuclear and conventional weapons, but this proposal has been stymied by the West's antecedent commitment to balance between conventional forces in the European theater.

7. Harold Brown, *Department of Defense Annual Report For FY 1979*, U.S. Government, Washington, D.C., February 2, 1978, p. 68.

8. George Kennan, "On Nuclear War," *The New York Review of Books* 28, nos. 21 and 22, January 21, 1982, pp. 8 and 10.

9. In the aftermath of President Reagan's announcement to embark upon production and stockpiling of the neutron bomb, no adequate explanation has been offered of the manner in which such enhanced radiation weapons can actually improve nuclear deterrence. In fact such weapons can only enhance deterrence if the Soviet Union believes American leadership to be *irrational*. This is the case because the first use of neutron weapons by the United States would carry a very high probability of unacceptably damaging nuclear counterretaliation by the Soviet Union. Should the Soviet leadership actually display this belief, then it would be decidedly irrational for them to initiate conventional conflict. Rather, the requirements of rational action would compel them to use nuclear weapons in any initial offensive move of war against an ally of the United States. It follows that the decision to produce the neutron bomb is, like all other associated elements of American nuclear strategy, entirely counterproductive to the security interests of the United States.

There are those who will argue that an American neutron bomb can enhance Western deterrence even if the Soviet leadership believes its American counterparts to be rational. This argument is founded upon the presumption that in the Soviet view American leaders do not believe that their first use of neutron weapons would draw a Soviet nuclear response. Yet all that is known about current Soviet nuclear strategy offers no reason whatever to accept this presumption. However, even if Soviet leaders believe that their American counterparts are rational but foolhardy, subject to unusual risk-taking behavior, they will still be confronted with conditions that encourage Soviet nuclear first use. It follows that even if we accept the assumption that the Soviet leadership perceives the American national command authority to be rational, the deployment of the neutron bomb by the United States would carry high costs and no benefits.

Of course, the dangers of the neutron bomb stem not only from Soviet perceptions of its hazards but also from the object of these perceptions, American nuclear strategy. Since the United States may believe that the first use of neutron weapons would entail a lower risk of escalation than other theater nuclear forces, it is more likely to initiate nuclear conflict because of these weapons. This heightened willingness to cross the firebreak between conventional and nuclear conflict greatly increases the likelihood of all-out nuclear war.

10. The need for such efforts is acknowledged by the authors of a recent report by the Directors of Forschungsinstitut der Deutschen Gessellschaft für Auswärtige Politik (Bonn); Council on Foreign Relations (New York); Institut Français des Relations Internationales (Paris); and Royal Institute

of International Affairs (London). See Karl Kaiser, Winston Lord, Thierry De Montbrial, and David Watt, *Western Security: What Has Changed? What Should Be Done?* (New York: Council on Foreign Relations 1981), p.27.

11. George H. Quester, "Arms Control: Toward Informal Solutions," in *Cruise Missiles: Technology, Strategy, Politics*, edited by Richard K. Betts (Washington, D.C.: The Brookings Institution, 1981), pp. 298–99.

12. The text of these pledges can be found in *Nuclear Weapons, Report of the Secretary General*, (Brookline, Mass: Autumn Press, 1980), pp. 178–79.

13. Alfonso Garcia Robles, "The Latin American Nuclear Weapon Free Zone," Stanley Foundation, Occasional Paper 19, May 1979, Muscatine, Iowa, p.20.

14. Bernard Gwertzman, "U.S. Starts Seeking Mideast Atom Ban," *The New York Times,* August 14, 1981, p. 1.

15. Comments in *New Outlook* (May 1982) special issue on "The Dangers of Nuclear Proliferation and Confrontation."

16. William Irwin Thompson, *Passages about Earth: An Exploration of the New Planetary Culture* (New York: Harper & Row, 1974), pp. 131–32.

17. See Grenville Clark and Louis B. Sohn, *World Peace through World Law*, 3rd ed. (Cambridge, Mass.: Harvard University Press, 1966), p. xi.

18. Early in 1977 the Carter administration undertook a detailed interagency review of unresolved SALT issues. In the hope of reaching significant strategic arms limitations, Secretary of State Vance and Ambassador Paul Warnke presented a comprehensive proposal to the Soviet Union in March 1977 that called for major cuts in the Vladivostok ceilings, as well as limits on the number of land-based ICBMs equipped with MIRVs and the number of very large, or "heavy," ICBMs. The proposal, which also called for restrictive limits on the testing and deployment of new types of ICBMs, was rejected by the USSR, as was an alternate deferral proposal under which the SALT II agreement would be based upon the Vladivostok numbers. In the Soviet view, both proposals were inconsistent with the agreement at Vladivostok.

19. See address by George F. Kennan on the occasion of his receiving the Albert Einstein Peace Prize, May 19, 1981 in *East/West Outlook* 4 no. 3 (July/August 1981), 4. Published by American Committee on East/West Accord. Reprinted with permission. Mr. Kennan's proposal can also be found in *The New York Review of Books* 28 no. 12, July 16, 1981, pp. 14–16.

20. Ironically, however, Kennan's proposal enjoys substantial public support in the United States according to a December 1981 Gallup poll. The survey found that by a margin of 4 to 1, Americans would support a

reduction by 50 percent in nuclear arms by the United States and the USSR. By 9 to 1, Americans would favor establishment of an international inspection agency to monitor such an arms reduction.

21. Robert C. Johansen, *Toward a Dependable Peace: A Proposal for an Appropriate Security System,* Working Paper no. 8., World Order Models Project, pp. 21–22.

22. Special consideration might be given to Secretary-General Waldheim's proposal during the tenth special session of the U.N. General Assembly that one-tenth of 1 percent of the annual world arms budget be spent on a campaign to mobilize world public opinion "on behalf of disarmament."

23. Richard Falk, "Normative Initiatives and Demilitarization: A Third System Approach," *Alternatives: A Journal of World Policy* 6, no. 2 (July 1980): 339–356.

24. Ibid., pp. 343–44.

25. Ibid., p. 343.

26. Ibid., p. 348.

27. See Arthur Koestler, *Janus: A Summing Up* (New York: Random House, 1978).

Index

About the Author

Louis René Beres, professor of political science at Purdue University, received the Ph.D. at Princeton University in 1971. A specialist in foreign affairs and international law with particular reference to strategic and world-order studies, he is the author of many major books and articles in the field. A frequent lecturer in the U.S. and abroad on matters concerning nuclear weapons and nuclear war, Professor Beres is an active member of such organizations as Physicians For Social Responsibility; The Committee for National Security; The American Committee for East/West Accord and the Institute for World Order's World Order Models Project. In recognition of this role in the worldwide movement against nuclear war, *The New York Times* recently described Dr. Beres's work as "one of the five leading "philosophical underpinnings" of that movement.